THE
NOW
SHOW
BOOK

THE NOW SHOW BOOK

★ ★ ★

HUGH DENNIS
STEVE PUNT
JON HOLMES

WITH
MARCUS BRIGSTOCKE
& MITCH BENN

An Orion paperback

First published in Great Britain in 2009 as *The Now Show Book of World Records* by Orion
This paperback edition published in 2010 by Orion Books Ltd, Orion House, 5 Upper St Martin's Lane, London WC2H 9EA

An Hachette UK company

10 9 8 7 6 5 4 3 2 1

A CIP catalogue record for this book is available from the British Library.

ISBN 978 1 4091 1754 4

Desig
Printe

The C   l,
renev   ıstainable
forest   MB   nform
to the

www.

DEDICATION

Steve would like to thank the islanders of Huik, the tiny Scottish island to which he retreated to write this book. It was they who stopped him at the harbour, and told him to 'Get yeself home and dinnae bring your indulgent pretensions round here. Have you nae got a Starbucks near your hoose?'

Hugh would like to dedicate this book to Deidre, Angus and Ezekiel but won't because he has no idea who they are and it would upset his wife Kate, and children Freddie and Meg.

Jon would like to thank father Pod, mother Homily, sister Arrietty and the rest of the Borrowers. He'll be back home soon, once he's stolen something useful from the big people. He dedicates his bits of the book to his wife Nicki and his daughter Maisie, who are both of normal size, and to be honest only took him home and adopted him because the zoo had run out of otters.

CONTENTS

INTRODUCTION

The authors have written this book in the expectation that it will become a key work of reference for families all over Britain. It has been painstakingly researched and assembled in order to provide clear and concise answers to the great questions of this, or any other age. It provides an invaluable addition to the library of any individual, university or institution, and it is hoped that it may come to replace the National Curriculum as the basis for teaching in all the schools of the United Kingdom. It is also hoped that a copy of this book may be placed in any future space probe so that occupants of other planets may come to understand our Earth. Plans are also under way to slip one into the bedside table of every hotel room on the planet, and selected copies will be left on trains and in taxis up and down the country, to make it look like it has government approval.

The authors generally take collective responsibility for the entries and their content, although in certain instances entries are individually attributed. This is usually because the views expressed are purely those of the author in question, and the rest of the team have no desire to be associated with the libellous rantings of their colleague. In other cases, the views expressed are clearly personal to the author, and everyone else has said 'Good grief. Can we make it clear I didn't say that? My family will never speak to me again.' In a few cases the others have threatened to resign unless 'that lunatic owns up'.

The key to individual attribution is as follows:

   SP Steve Punt
   HD Hugh Dennis
   JH Jon Holmes

   with
   MB Mitch Benn
   MB Marcus Brigstocke.

So, all in all, not a suitable system, really.

MODERN
SOCIETY,
PUBLIC

BIGGEST SCARE STORY

The media love a scare story, and time and time again, we all fall for it. There is one thing you need to remember at all times – *most media people have arts-subject degrees*. They know about English, media studies or socioeconomics. They do not generally know *anything* about science, and they do not generally understand much maths beyond GCSE. If they did, they'd have better paid jobs in banks or investment companies.

With this in mind, you can start enjoying the spectacularly stupid way the media tend to cover scientific and medical stories. You will also find you don't spend the whole time panicking and worrying, which is good for your blood pressure. Here are some familiar headlines . . .

LARGE HADRON COLLIDER WILL DESTROY THE WORLD!!!
Most people don't know what a hadron is, let alone what happens when you collide them (see SCIENTIFIC THEORY, MOST INCOMPREHENSIBLE). This led to a lot of stuff in the papers about how a particle accelerator in Switzerland would create mini-black holes which would devour the planet. I have a friend who studied physics at university, and I asked him about this. He just rolled his eyes. It was cobblers.

TERRIFYING DISEASE WILL KILL HALF THE POPULATION!!!
When I was a student in the mid-80s, I walked past a newsagents one morning and our best-selling Sunday broadsheet was leading on a headline that said 'By the Year 2000, One-Third of the Population Will Have Herpes'. If there was one section of the population this should have put the wind up, it was students, but everybody just went 'Huh?' It was obvious rubbish, and has

been repeated many times since. In 1996 we were told that, by
now, a third of us would be dying of Creuzfeldt-Jakob disease.
A few years later we were all going to die of SARS. A few years
ago we were going to be decimated by bird flu, a disease which
doesn't actually exist yet (the human-communicable version
being a theoretical mutation). The bird flu scare was centred
around chickens; swine flu around pigs. We seem to be working
our way through the cast of 'Old MacDonald had a farm'. Next
year we'll probably all be terrified of sheep bloat.

MILLENNIUM BUG WILL KILL MILLIONS!!

Physics, epidemiology; what we don't understand, we get scared
by. Computers are another thing we don't really understand
and, sure enough, in 1999 along came a computer scare story.
We were solemnly warned that computers wouldn't be able to
recognise the change to the year 2000; they'd all assume it was
the year 1900, and turn themselves into manual typewriters
with a gas-lamp attached.

The effects of this, we were solemnly warned, would be
catastrophic: planes would fall from the sky, hospitals would
switch themselves off, electricity grids would fail. Computer
experts vainly tried to explain this wasn't true, but the
cacophony of morons was so loud that they gave up and decided
instead they might as well make some money out of it. So they
started charging governments and companies a fortune to make
sure they were 'YK2 compliant'. Hundreds of millions of pounds
were spent. I spent an amusing afternoon on the internet in
late 1999, surfing American evangelist sites selling Y2K survival
videos.

In the event, the only computer-based thing that happened
was that on 31 December 1999, the stock market reached its
highest-ever peak; it has never been near it since, and a decade

later (at the time of writing), it is at less than two-thirds of where it was ten years ago. Which makes you wonder whether the only effect of the Millennium Bug was to introduce a virus that would suddenly value dot-com companies at a realistic level.

MOST POPULAR NETWORKING WEBSITE

MitchBenn The most popular networking website in the world is currently Twitter, with a global membership in excess of nine million.
20.20 29 May 2009 from web

MitchBenn Since its creation by Jack Dorsey in 2006, Twitter has been used for social purposes, marketing, political advertising and entertainment.
20.21 29 May 2009 from web

MitchBenn Twitter's appeal is based on its simplicity; members post short messages of no more than 140 characters each (including spaces).
20.22 29 May 2009 from web

MitchBenn While the 140-character limit encourages brevity and conciseness it can be annoying when you're in the middle of something and you run out o
20.24 29 May 2009 from web

MitchBenn Sorry . . . Like I said, it can be annoying when you run out of characters just as you're about to make an important point, or trying to develo
20.25 29 May 2009 from web

MitchBenn Oh FFS. Look, it's fun but limiting. Will that do?
I suppose I could mention the whole King of Twitter thing.
Why not? Yes.

20.26 29 May 2009 from web

MitchBenn In 2009, Mitch Benn from BBC Radio 4's *The Now
Show* attempted to usurp @stephenfry from his position as
Britain's most popular Twitterer.

20.28 29 May 2009 from web

punty You're not still on about this, are you?

20.29 29 May 2009 from BBCnet

MitchBenn Reasoning that if all 2 million *Now Show* listeners
could be persuaded to 'follow' him on the site he would become
the most followed person o

20.31 29 May 2009 from web

punty Whose idea was it to get Mitch to write the Twitter entry
anyway?

20.32 29 May 2009 from web

MitchBenn BOLLOCKS – most followed Twitterer. The plan's
ultimate failure was the result of the apathy, Luddism &
technophobia of the British people.

20.33 29 May 2009 from web

HimOffOutnumbered I think he rather took it upon himself,
didn't he?

20.34 29 May 2009 from BBCnet

MitchBenn But my time will come! The day will dawn when all
will quail before me as the Master of the Twitterverse! Bwaa ha
ha ha ha ha ha ha ha h

20.36 29 May 2009 from web

punty He's off his meds again. Hold him down!

20.37 29 May 2009 from BBCnet

jonholmes1 YOU bloody hold him down.

20.38 29 May 2009 from HobbitWeb

MitchBenn Mad? Mad?! TheY saId eiNstEin wAs mAd! theY sAid cHarLes MaNson was maD! I'Ll sHow yOU! i'lL ShOw yoU aLlÖ

20.40 29 May 2009 from web

stephenfry MITCH BENN . . .?

20.41 29 May 2009 from Fryberry

MitchBenn No! No!

20.41 29 May 2009 from web

stephenfry Silence! End this foolishness and pester these good readers no more with your folderol and gimcrackery! BEGONE, I say! BEGONE!

20.42 29 May 2009 from Fryberry

MitchBenn Noooooooooooooooooooooooooooooooooooooooooooooo ooooooooooooo . . .

20.42 29 May 2009 from web

punty Gosh, thank you, Stephen Fry.

20.43 29 May 2009 from BBCnet

stephenfry I'm sorry you had to witness such unpleasantries, my darlings. I now return you to the welcoming embrace of this wholly delightful book.

20.44 29 May 2009 from Fryberry

MB

MOST RECOGNISABLE NEWSPAPER EDITORIAL STYLE

Style – as Aristotle opined – is what is left when fashion has passed; and in the face of such time-honoured Hellenic wisdom, who are we to disagree? It is interesting to note, therefore, that in this age of iPods and Twitters (whatever they may be!), it is essential (in its original Platonic sense) that the tradition of over-written, sub-clause-laden, polysyllabic thickets of verbiage be upheld by the leader column of the broadsheet press. Both the *Daily Telegraph* and *The Times* adhere fastidiously to this convention, deploying an impressive arsenal of long words and, *inter alia*, legalistic terms and foreign usages to thicken the mixture, whether the required tone be one of *joie de vivre* or of *weltshmertz*. The editorial column will invariably end in a long, measured sentence with a semi-colon in it; it is this closing cadence which, as Dr Johnson said, elevates quotidian thought into ineffable, gnomic truth. Long may it continue.

SECOND MOST RECOGNISABLE NEWSPAPER EDITORIAL STYLE

GIVE US A BREAK! The posh papers can prattle on all they want, but the average hard-working family has no time for the Oxbridge elites in their ivory towers! That's why the *Sun* says you can stuff your long-winded editorials up your Court Circular! The man in the street wants plain-speaking truth, so they can tell their hard-working families how Great Britain is being dragged down by the so-called liberal elite, who, along with the PC brigade and the fat cat BBC, have done so much to turn us into the laughing stock of Europe! Not that we mind – we hate Europe!

THIRD MOST RECOGNISABLE NEWSPAPER EDITORIAL STYLE

It was the Conservatives under Thatcher who, through their consistent assault on the public-service sector, consistently undermined and denigrated the teaching profession, turning the acquisition of literacy into a target-based political football. It was also under the Tories that children were forced to share textbooks, to be force-fed chips and pizza instead of nutritious rice and grains, and to suffer cruel beatings at the hands of sadistic headmasters who, egged on by their supporters in the Tory press, advocated the use of the cane, the thumbscrew, and waterboarding for late homework. Sadly, Labour failed to reform all of these Tory measures, due to Tony Blair's general self-righteous uselessness. The result of this is that the *Guardian* can go back to doing what it does best – blaming the Conservatives for everything. In the words of the great social reformer Nathaniel Dogoodier: 'The working class are splendid. Everyone else is evil and wrong.' Amen to that.

THE RECORD FOR THE MOST STUPID THING EVER SAID IN A NEWSPAPER . . .

. . . Is in today's *Daily Mail*. Mercifully this fact remains perpetually true as the editorial commitment to one-sided ignorance and wholesale stupidity means that each day sees new lows for Paul Dacre and his legion of dolts. MB

MOST LITIGIOUS COMPANY

The world's most litigious company is XXXX, who have no sense of humour at all. The slightest joke about their XXX, or their revolting XXXX, or the way their staff are threatened with XXX if they try to XXXX, will result in the threat of libel actions. They have bullied and hounded dozens of TV shows and newspapers into dropping jokes about them; the BBC is petrified of XXXX, but then, the BBC is petrified of everybody. Well, we're not going to be intimidated by multi-national bully-boys and their fat pompous lawyers. We say – (THIS SECTION DELETED). And furthermore, they can (THIS SECTION DELETED).

MOST COVETED AWARD

There are awards for virtually everything, but the officially most coveted award is still the Nobel Prize. These were established in 1901 at the behest of Alfred Nobel, inventor of the door knocker. It replaced the previous set of awards for excellence in various fields of academe and science, the Mister Clever Pants Awards. The Nobels retain their prestige even though they are not televised and do not attract big celebrities. ITV have proposed a ceremony called the 'People's Nobels', to be presented to 'boffins and brainboxes whose crazy ideas have changed the world!!'. Richard Hammond will present, with Fearne Cotton backstage asking the winners 'how it felt when all those long hours in the laboratory paid off '.

The complete list of Nobel Prizes is as follows:

Physics / Chemistry / Medicine / Literature / Peace / Economics / Baking / Pedantry / Gurning / Sloth / Avarice / Sarcasm

The first winner of the Nobel Prize for Sarcasm was a James Henley of Wolverhampton (but not *the* James Henley of Wolverhampton). Upon hearing of his award, he is reported to have said: 'Oh well that's just *great*, isn't it?'

The most controversial award in the history of the Nobel Prize was the presentation in 1999 of the Nobel Peace Prize to Vinnie Jones. While this has been proven to have been the result of a typographical error, no one has ever had the balls to attempt to retrieve the prize.

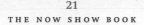

MOST-REPEATED SHOWBIZ MYTH THAT CAN'T BE SPECIFIED FOR LEGAL REASONS

1 Marc Almond and the stomach pump

2 Why they're called the Pet Shop Boys

3 Richard Gere and the hamster (See also 2.)

4 Marianne Faithfull and the Mars bar

5 Why they are called 10cc (See also 1.)

MOST EYEBROW-RAISING THING BLAMED ON THE CREDIT CRUNCH

Recently all world records have been broken for using a single excuse for everything. The credit crunch has been held to blame for all of the following:

- Closure of rabbit-selling business

- Lack of big-money signings at Portsmouth FC

- Cancellation of *The Bill*

- Fewer pensioners going on outings

- 'The breakdown of trust in society'*

That one was the Church. The same Church that previously said 'the breakdown in trust in society' came from too much affluence.

- Divorces
- Babies
- Lower prawn prices
- Drop in sales of flat-pack houses
- Drop in sales of any houses
- Loss of eyesight
  (people avoiding check-ups to save money)
- Racism at football grounds
  (connection unclear here)
- Being caught driving without insurance
  (man claimed he couldn't afford policy renewal)
- Bring caught drink-driving
  (estate agent claimed stress drove him to pub after work)
- Fewer people using public transport
- Too many people using public transport
- Mugging
- Domestic violence
- Music festivals cancelled
  (don't worry, there are still plenty left)
- Children not having school meals
- Rise in anti-depressant prescriptions
- Squatters moving into listed buildings
- Chimney fires as people cut down on central heating

- Theft of some koi carp in Burnley

- Theft of all kinds

- Massive rise in Robert Peston-related incidents

The current record, though, is held by a report which claimed that: 'The credit crunch is being blamed for forcing mortgage lenders to reduce the amount they will lend to house buyers.' Thing is – that's what a credit crunch *is*. That's the *definition* of a credit crunch. Which means that the credit crunch is even to blame for itself.

ODDEST ELECTION RESULT ANNOUNCEMENT

When a new Pope is elected, all the cardinals of the Roman Catholic Church are locked in the Sistine Chapel at the Vatican and are not let out until they have decided who should get the job, or at least until Tom Hanks has been able to run round Rome a bit. The decision is made by voting in a series of secret ballots until a single candidate manages to secure the required number of votes, the result of each ballot being announced by the colour of smoke emerging from a chimney above the chapel. Dark smoke signals that no Pope has been chosen, while white smoke signifies that a new Pope has been elected. (Green smoke indicates that Damien has fulfilled The Omen and that the apocalpyse is nigh.) The total election can take several days, during which time the cardinals have very little to do except stare at the ceiling, which is probably why Michelangelo made it so interesting up there.

The system of smoke signals has also led to a few false alarms. During the election of the most recent Pope, Cardinal Ratzinger (Pope Benedict XVI), the result of the second ballot was interrupted by the environmental health department wanting to know why the cardinals weren't using Coalite as stipulated in an urban area. The smoke from the third ballot was of an uncertain colour and carried the faint but suspicious smell of sausages, and after the fourth ballot, the smoke signals inadvertently spelt out.

'White man he come this way with 50 horses, maybe 60. Gather um braves, scalp him and steal his um fire-water.'

Given that the average age of the 115 cardinals is around 80, it is hardly surprising that when Ratzinger was finally elected, the emergence of the white smoke was also accompanied by the sounds of grumpy scuffles as 114 of the cardinals berated their one neighbour who had lit a bonfire for the fifth time that weekend.

MOST OUTRAGEOUS MPS' EXPENSES CLAIMS

We all thought expenses scandals were over with the arrival of a new government. Turned out they weren't. So here's a few of the all-time favourites:

Hubert Munnygrabb, MP for Nottreel South, constructed a full-scale Roman bath in his garden, including a steam room and mosaic-floored caldarium with marble benches and a full-time masseur. He claimed the entire cost back, saying that it was regularly used for his constituency surgeries. Asked to justify the salaries paid to the two semi-naked dancing girls who were employed to carry jugs of cold water to the bathers, he said that they 'helped his constituents to put their problems in perspective'.

Lady Lavinia Fleecey, MP for Soke-le-Taxpaier, bought a racehorse called Chandler's Ford and trained him for the Derby. She put this on expenses, claiming that she was 'intending to distribute the winnings to constituency charities'.

Barry Brazen, MP for Duckin and Divin West, bought £400 of take-away curry for all his mates one Saturday night and charged it to the taxpayer, claiming it was 'valuable input to the local economy'.

Nathan Pratten-Whittney, MP for Twattleton, bought an early Matisse at auction at Sotheby's. He paid £3.4 million for it and hung it in his house, claiming it was to 'entice burglars and thereby demonstrate the effectiveness of the local police force'.

LEAST OUTRAGEOUS MPS' EXPENSES CLAIM

In 2009 the British Parliament almost collapsed when it was discovered that everyone who worked there as an MP was found to be spending public money on lifestyles that would make even Elton John think he was overdoing it a bit, and ought to rein it in. A leak to the *Daily Telegraph* provided evidence that Douglas Hogg used £2,000 of taxpayers' money to have Alan Duncan cleaned, Sir Michael Spicer paid £6,000 for a tonne of Hazel Blears's manure so that he could grow his own chandeliers on a tennis court, while Sir Peter Viggers had built a Michael Martin House on a small island where he keeps the former Speaker of the House for his eggs. Meanwhile, Shahid Malik was caught buying a mock-tudor flat-screen trouser press for his constituency piano and then we discovered that in fact *all* MPs had, for many years, been lifting their middle fingers at the electorate and then 'flipping' them in a practice known as 'telling the electorate to eff off'.

But while public attention and anger turned quite rightly to these extravagances, the MPs who had played by the rules, who hadn't been coining it from the public purse, received scant attention. Some MPs didn't claim for anything. Not all of them were on the make, and thus it would be unfair to tar all MPs with the brush that says they are all a conniving, lying, fraudulent, unethical, devious, abhorrent, hypocritical, slimy, scum-sucking, rip-off bunch of disreputable twunts. So it's only right, fair and proper that we list here those MPs who, for the last few years, have not been on the take. And here they are. In the years 2002–2009, records show that no expenses whatsoever were claimed by the following Members of Parliament:

- Winston Churchill

- David Lloyd George

- Robin Cook

- Enoch Powell

- William Gladstone

- Pitt the Younger

- Pitt the Elder

- Pitt the Middle One That Felt Insecure About
  It And Had A Real Sense Of Not Belonging

- Viscount Palmerston

- Benjamin Disraeli

- Alan Clark

Records from the Members' Fees and Allowances Office
demonstrate that not one of these MPs claimed a penny in the
last six years because they were dead. Although when they were
alive, they were just as bad as the rest. A leak to *The Now Show
Book* shows that in the years 1939–1945, Churchill used public
money to get drunk on brandy, and while he was Lord Privy Seal,
the Right Honourable Pitt The Elder, the First Earl of Chatham
claimed expenses to stay in London instead of travelling back
to Chatham (allowable, however, on the grounds that no one
should have to go to Chatham). Enoch Powell spent £129,000
from the public purse on racism and back when Robin Cook
was alive, he used taxpayers' money to pay for the upkeep of
his second beard. In May 2010 all MPs were punished by not
one party getting enough votes to actually form a government.

Although as usual they ignored this and made one up anyway, one that no one wanted or had voted for. That's democracy, that is.

WORST US PRESIDENT

George W. Bush is universally recognised as the worst US President of all time, largely due to his 'shock and awe' tactics. In his first term, there was shock at the speed with which he pissed away the sympathy for 9/11; in the second term, awe as he oversaw the total collapse of the world economy.

MOST COMICAL PRIME MINISTERS

In the post-war period, satire began in 1961 when, famously, Peter Cook became the first person to impersonate a living Prime Minister on stage. Before this, though, Prime Ministers still had amusing attributes – some more so than others.

CLEMENT ATTLEE Elected in a landslide in 1945, he set up the NHS, nationalised a load of stuff and had the good fortune to live in an age when you weren't allowed to make jokes about politics.

WINSTON CHURCHILL Drank a lot. Chain-smoked. Refused to appear on television, which has kept his mystique going; your mental image of him will be from World War Two, when he was only in his 60s. By the time he was PM again in the 1950s, he was past his vote-by date, but no one dared to make jokes about him. This was not because he'd had a stroke in 1953 because that was kept secret. It was because people loved his funny car insurance ads.

ANTHONY EDEN Replaced Churchill in 1955 and, like all non-elected Prime Ministers, was swiftly punished. The Suez Crisis finished him off fast.

HAROLD MACMILLAN Doddery old aristocrat. Liked shooting grouse and watching the modern world pass by. Said 'you've never had it so good', but only after he'd nicked it from an American presidential campaign.

ALEC DOUGLAS-HOME Replaced Macmillan after the Profumo crisis. Like all non-elected Prime Ministers, he was swiftly punished. Ousted the following year by . . .

HAROLD WILSON Pipe-smoking, mac-wearing paranoid, convinced everyone was out to get him, including the BBC, MI5 and the press. Fortunately, he had Mike Yarwood to make him look lovable, when he wasn't at all. He was a grumpy conspiracy theorist, and if he were alive today, he'd probably write a blog for the *Daily Telegraph*.

EDWARD HEATH Possibly the most comical of all British Prime Ministers. He had a silly laugh, a funny voice, he played the organ, conducted orchestras, had a yacht and was a 'confirmed bachelor' who nevertheless managed to become Prime Minister. They don't make 'em like that any more.

JIM CALLAGHAN Genial 'sunny Jim', who has gone down in history as the man who flew back from holiday into strike-ridden Britain and said 'Crisis? What crisis?' He never, of course, said this at all; it was a *Sun* headline, nicked from the title of an album by Supertramp. What he actually said was: 'I'm saying nothing to you bloody journalists, you'll probably make something up based on the title of an album by some keyboard-based AOR band.'

Anyway, like all non-elected Prime Ministers, he was fairly swiftly punished, losing at the next ballot to . . .

MARGARET THATCHER Unlike Wilson and Heath, Thatcher did not inspire gentle mockery, but vitriolic hatred and an entire new genre of humour: 'alternative comedy'. This replaced jokes about fat mothers-in-law and stupid Irishmen with new jokes about fat yuppies and stupid policemen. Was directly responsible for the rise of Ben Elton. (See *MOST BAFFLINGLY SUCCESSFUL DREADFUL MUSICAL*.)

JOHN MAJOR A textbook example of how satire can get it totally wrong and still work. Major was depicted as grey, dull and humourless. He was, in fact, by all accounts rather witty and genial, and such was his gentlemanly charm that he had an affair with Edwina Currie. This was far funnier than anything the satirists ever invented about him, and I should know – I was one of them.

TONY BLAIR In 1997 everyone wondered how the leftie clique of so-called comedians would deal with having a Labour Prime Minister, let alone one whom everybody adored and whose approval ratings were sky-high. Fortunately, they swiftly realised that Blair was a vapid, empty, pompous, policyless, shameless warmongering arse, and this made him much funnier. And that was before he started grovelling to Silvio Berlusconi (see *POLITICIAN, WORLD'S FUNNIEST*). Berlusconi is right-wing, rich and [allegedly] borderline dodgy – but he had a nice big house, which was much more important to a Labour Prime Minister.

GORDON BROWN Like all non-elected Prime Ministers . . . let's not go there. Or indeed, to Rochdale. It's full of bigots, isn't it, Gordon?

DAVID CAMERON Ground-breaking in that he chose to work as half of a double act. It's the old straight-man/straight-man routine.

BIGGEST EROSIONS OF CIVIL LIBERTIES UNDER THE BLAIR / BROWN GOVERNMENT

- Rendition flights for anyone fishing without a valid permit.
- Waterboarding for anyone without a dog licence, but only if they're a Muslim, as technically dog licences were discontinued in 1987.
- If you try to rent a DVD from Blockbuster without having your membership card then you will be incarcerated without trial and then shot.

MOST POWERFUL EVIL SENTIENT FORCE THAT WILL PROBABLY TAKE OVER THE WORLD AND ENSLAVE ALL OF MANKIND

In reverse order of likeliness:

5 The Borg from *Star Trek*

4 Skynet from *The Terminator*

3 Starbucks

2 China

1 Tesco

BIGGEST MISTAKE BY LOW-RANKING GOVERNMENT OFFICIAL

Low-ranking government officials are always in trouble. Whenever a laptop containing sensitive information vital to national security is left on a train or in the back of a taxi, you can guarantee it'll have been left there by a 'low-ranking government official'. One has to wonder what a low-ranking government official is doing with such vitally sensitive information in the first place. *They simply shouldn't be given important things to take home.* When I was at school, anyone considered to be a low-ranking child wasn't even allowed to look after the guinea pig, and with good reason, so why don't the government follow this simple precedent?

The three biggest mistakes involving a low-ranking government official all occurred in 2008 when a junior civil servant left the then Work and Pensions Secretary Hazel Blears on a train; a worker at the Department of Culture, Media and Sport walked out of a bar leaving the site of the 2012 Olympic Stadium on a chair; the then Defence Secretary John Hutton left Big Ben in the back of a taxi after he'd been entrusted to take the clock home.

The biggest mistake by a low-ranking child was made at Jon's school by Paul Griffiths, aged eight, when he tried to clean the class guinea pig in his mum's washing machine at the setting for 90° minimum iron. JH

MOST POINTLESS INTER-GOVERNMENTAL ORGANISATION

There are many inter-governmental organisations, among them the G8 (a forum for the group of eight most industrialised nations), the G20 (a meeting of finance ministers from the 19 most industrialised nations and the EU), and the G45 (a group of hypo-allergenic countries that can be used on areas of eczema, scratches or dry and flaking skin). However, from a recent poll of people who think it is a bit pointless having an organisation that claims to be united when actually the members can't agree on anything, the most pointless inter-governmental organisation is the UNITED NATIONS. Set up in 1945 it may be the most ineffective organisation in human history, with the possible exception of Haringey Child Protection services.

There is one part within the organisation that stands out as monumentally ineffective however, namely the Security Council. The Security Council, although sounding like the trade body for alarm companies, is actually responsible for maintaining world peace. Whoops! It has five permanent members, China, France, Russia, Great Britain and the United States, these being countries that didn't lose WW2, and ten non-permanent members, rotated every two years on a regional basis, these being countries that are largely bitter and resentful at not being allowed to be there all the time but not big enough to start a war over it.

Nothing at all has been decided at the United Nations, ever. Debates also take twice as long as they should because everyone has to listen to a simultaneous translation of what is being said, although frankly if I was in the Russian delegation debating whether to severely sanction pant-suited Elvis nut-job Kim Jong-il over his nuclear missile tests, when I knew that Russia had supplied him with most of his nuclear hardware in the first place, I wouldn't bother to listen anyway.

BEST METHOD OF CELEBRATING THE FOUNDING OF THE EUROPEAN UNION

The year 2004 saw the 50th anniversary of the signing of the Treaty of Rome – the document which set up the pre-cursor to the pre-cursor of the European Union, the European Coal and Steel Community. German Chancellor Angela Merkel commissioned a birthday card, the wording of which was only revealed at the very last minute so that the other countries wouldn't have a chance to veto it. And what did the continent that produced Cervantes, Balzac, Shakespeare, Goethe, Dante, Ibsen, Sven Hassel and the bloke who created Tintin come up with? Well, after much discussion the official birthday greeting turned out to be:

Together. For 50 years.

Yes. It took almost six countries to come up with nearly one word each. Each nation was also invited to celebrate the event. Britain typically didn't bother, but across the rest of the Union they really let their imaginations run wild. Here are a few countries and their chosen method of celebration:*

Belgium: *A rock concert fronted by Kim Wilde*
She had a number one there apparently, although to be honest that isn't really that much of an achievement. I've had one there too, the coach stopped there so we could all have one.

All true, even the one about the circular walk.

Ireland: *Special European-themed church services*
Presumably incorporating the following reading – 'Jesus wanted
to feed the 5,000, but could gather only five loaves and the two
fishes left in the Sea of Galilee once the Spanish trawlers had
finished with it. Luckily, there was a French farmer in the crowd
and he'd been paid loads of money to grow far too much wheat,
so in the end there was a loaf each. God bless the EU. Now if they
could only force Bono to pay his tax.'

Denmark: *Every citizen was given a free bun*
Yes, that was what the founders dreamed of. A continent twice
shattered by war, its soil drenched with the blood of its people,
its great cathedrals lying in ruins, but they dared to dream that
one day, one glorious day, there'd be free buns for all. They were,
however, specially themed buns, designed to be ceremonially
recalled when it was realised that they didn't conform to the
EU's bun circumference directive.

Luxembourg: *Citizens were encouraged to go on a circular walk*
If you live in Luxembourg and like walking, a circular walk is
pretty much all you can do anyway. If, for example, you ran a
half-marathon you would end up in Belgium, and if there were
too many of you it would count as an invasion, which might not
have been the best way of celebrating European unity.

Estonia: *Trees were planted*
Big Leylandii along the border, to annoy Latvia

Spain: *Students built a giant puzzle of the 27 countries*
To start with they got it wrong, but realised when they found
they had put Britain at the heart of Europe.

Cyprus: *Their European Union office had an open day*
What a celebration that was. Your chance to photocopy your
arse on the taxpayer.

Romania: *Hosted an internet chat room*
Where unsuspecting children could be groomed by Europhiles.

Slovenia: *Held a parachute jump*
Unfortunately for those on the jump the decision to pull the
cord had to be ratified by all 27 parachutists. Each parachutist
could make the case for pulling, or not pulling, the cord, and
these statements were then considered as part of an ongoing
process, which they hoped would lead to a cord-pulling
agreement within an 18-month period.

MOST WORRYING ASPECT
OF A GREATER EMPHASIS
ON NUCLEAR POWER

To satisfy the nation's ever-increasing demand for electricity,
while at the same time reducing carbon emissions, it is now
planned to replace our coal- and gas-fired power stations with a
new generation of nuclear reactors. This obviously raises many
issues of public safety. We are told, however, that these dangers
will be minimised by placing the new facilities in 'remote rural
areas where not many people live'.

Rather than being reassuring, this is perhaps the most
worrying aspect of the whole proposal. If a nuclear power plant
is to be placed in a remote rural area where not many people live,

does this not mean that they will have to recruit their staff from remote rural areas where not many people live?

The staffing situation in other countries is no less serious. According to the *Sunday Times*, after the Israeli attack on their nuclear reactor in 1981, it was neither Iranian scientists nor politicians who decided to disperse the Iranian nuclear power plants around the country, but rather the mullahs, or men of God. One can only hope that putting religious leaders in charge of the power companies isn't a trend that catches on in the UK. Our power companies are privatised and ultra-competitive.

Transcript: the *Today* programme

JOHN HUMPHRIES: And this morning on Thought for the Day it is the Rt Rev Richard Harries, Bishop of Oxford.

REV HARRIES: Thank you, John. Have you ever thought, I wonder, of changing your electricity supplier? Come to the Church of England for both electricity and gas and you could get a 15 per cent discount and preferential entry to the kingdom of heaven.

BEST SOLUTION TO GLOBAL WARMING AS YET INEXPLICABLY IGNORED BY GOVERNMENT

Much of the electricity we consume, and therefore much of the carbon we burn, is used to provide light in our homes, offices, streets and schools, throughout the hours of darkness. Hence the new coalition government's desire that we all switch to low-voltage bulbs from the traditional incandescent variety. Indeed, like a working majority under the first-past-the-post electoral system, incandescent bulbs will soon be impossible to obtain. Yet while the government say they are keen to investigate all possible routes to a low-carbon future, they seem to have overlooked a solution which would mean that we needed no bulbs at all, and yet were still able to go about our business in perfect comfort and safety.

Night-vision goggles.
Think about it: if every family in Britain were issued with a set of night-vision goggles, each and every bulb in Britain could be switched off, including all street lighting and those illuminating the motorway network. There is of course a cost implication – they are expensive at around £500 a pair – but a bulk order of 60 million would surely generate some sort of discount. Against this must be counted a vast saving in electricity, and the fact that if we reduce carbon usage we are saving the planet, and thus the human race, probably. Think of the children. What is more, there would be an unexpected fillip for manufacturing (albeit the arms industry), a boost for opticians providing lenses in the

goggles for the short-sighted, and the thrill for the wearer of feeling that they are living in an action movie. It is a win–win situation. Night-vision goggles – the Green alternative the Blues and Yellows have ignored.

LEAST FLEXIBLE CLASS SYSTEM – THE FRENCH

Britain has a reputation as one of the most class-orientated societies on earth, and you can understand why. For centuries we have had an unelected second chamber where the upper echelons of the aristocracy come to sleep in comfortable surroundings, while next door, our elected representatives debate the great issues of the day: could a new Range Rover count as a second home if you fall asleep in it occasionally? Could porn films be made to appear as something else on a monthly statement from Virgin Mobile? Clearly this class distinction between the two great Chambers has long been thought unacceptable, which is why, post the election of 2010 and the rise of 'new politics', the system was reformed by making the elected Cabinet significantly posher than the Lords next door. The class system is also a major part of our appeal to tourists, who like nothing more than to watch the pomp associated with our monarchy; the changing of the guard and the Duke of Edinburgh being deliberately insulting to foreigners. The system seems old and intransigent, and yet no one has ever bothered to try and change or do away with it, and Britain has never had a revolution. Now admittedly that is partly because we are a deeply un-revolutionary people

given to muttering under our breath rather than taking to
the barricades, which is of course why a British version of *Les
Misérables* would be exactly that, miserable, with no singing
and no shouting, just a cast tutting loudly.

There is, however, another reason for the class system's
survival: the fact that the system is actually very fluid. For
example, during the industrial revolution, if you happened
to find coal on your land, or were very good at building canals,
or filthy rich through getting your hands dirty in some other
way, the likelihood was that you would be offered some sort of
peerage. This has, of course, remained a feature of British life
right up until last year when a Metropolitan Police investigation
found that it wasn't. Honestly, they really didn't find anything
dodgy at all.

By contrast, the French aristocracy were rather less flexible,
indeed the least flexible. To join their club you had to have a
blood test, and if it turned out to be anything other than a really
deep shade of blue there was no way you were getting in. As a
result, your average upwardly mobile French peasant was given
no choice but to apply to the local socialist council for a grant
to buy a guillotine.

It was a very short-sighted move, frankly. Yes, they got a
musical out of it – for which Cameron Mackintosh was knighted,
just to infuriate the French – but they haven't got a version of *To
the Manor Born*, and *Upstairs Downstairs* made very little sense in
Clermont-Ferrand.

MOST HATED CORPORATE JARGON

All corporate jargon is hated, but at present, the most especially loathed clichés seem to be:

Let's get our ducks in a row on this
A metaphor based on those fairground shooting games. It would make sense if it meant 'Let's pick off a series of easy targets' but it doesn't, it means 'Let's do things in a logical sequence'. So it doesn't even make sense. Fairground ducks are already in a row, they're stuck to a conveyor belt, for God's sake. Unless, of course, it refers to real ducks. Getting real ducks into a row would be very difficult, as they are wild creatures and don't really take instructions. Therefore it would mean 'This is an impossible task, akin to trying to teach waterfowl to form a queue'.

You've got to step up to the plate
An American phrase, annoyingly used by idiots in this country. It comes from baseball, and means nothing at all in Britain. The correct version would be 'You've got to put down your sandwich and walk out to the wicket'.

We need to incentivise the customer
In English, this phrase should be 'We've got to give customers an incentive' – but never underestimate the capacity of the verbally challenged to want to de-noun everything and verbiate it instead. Even once turned into a verb, a word isn't safe – sometimes it gets turned into a longer verb just for the sake of it. This is why Americans don't get burgled – they get 'burglarised'. This creates problems for police spokesmen, who have to explain

that they are trying to catch the burglarisator in an attempt to bring down the local burglarisation rate. President Obama recently announced an anti-burglary scheme as 'a new plan to de-burglarizationalise America'.

We intend to action this going forward
'Actioning', like 'incentivising' is a horrible word, but it does save time if you're too lazy to say 'put into action', which, after all, takes ages to say. 'Going forward' is currently in the Top 5 Most Hated Phrases in Britain   polls for both the *Daily Telegraph* and the BBC have proved this. Apart from anything else, the nature of reality precludes any alternative to going forward. To go anywhere other than forward would involve the total rewriting of all known laws of the physical universe. What takes the phrase beyond irritating and into the realm of twitching, gibbering rage is when it is used by politicians to mean 'let's change the subject'. A typical exchange will go like this –

INTERVIEWER: So, Minister   do you accept that you made a massive cock-up that has cost the taxpayer millions of pounds?

POLITICIAN: Well, I think that going forward there are lessons we can learn . . .

– in other words, *I'm admitting nothing and clinging on to my job and, in fact, I've done everyone a favour by exposing flaws in the system. In fact, you should be thanking me, really. Thanks to my massive cock-up, future generations will be spared the same thing happening to them! That's how public-spirited I am! I deserve a knighthood!*

WORST
POLITICAL GAFFE

Lembit Opik.

MOST LIKELY PHRASES
OF CORPORATE JARGON
TO ANNOY YOU IN FUTURE

Corporate jargon changes very quickly, and while this book was in production, the following phrases have appeared on the radar –

1 'Appearing on the radar'

2 'I'm going to run these ideas into the sky and then water them through a thought box until they shout "teamwork"'

3 'Let's rocket the salad on that'

4 'I only want ideas that are amphibious. Go!'

5 'This horizontal display artifice goes live to dialogue at 9 a.m.'
   (Translation: This shelf needs to be stacked with tins of pet food by the time the supermarket opens.)

6 'I don't want to drill down the whole department over in-house core competency and thus implement a blamestorm vis-à-vis the rolling out of product – but which one of you has been putting two gherkins instead of one in the double whoppers?'

·· ☠ ··

WORST NAME FOR A CAR COMPANY WISHING TO CONVINCE INVESTORS OF ITS LONG-TERM PROSPECTS IN AN ECONOMIC DOWNTURN

TATA.

MOST HATED MADE-UP WORD

All the words we actually need were invented centuries ago, when people would make new words by putting two other words together – but in Latin or Greek, so it at least sounded like a proper word. Famously, the word 'television' has half from each language, which 1920s' pedant C.P. Snow didn't like; but what, then, would he have made of *staycation*, a made up word that means 'not going on holiday'; and what would he have made of *guesstimate*, a word which is much hated even by the sort of people who don't normally hate made-up words. Most of us can put up with *blogging* or *googling* in the same way we put up with *scuba* or *radar*; acronyms and contractions have always given us useful new words. Even the word *wags* as in wives and girlfriends of footballers, has proved useful. But words which regularly top polls of Most Hated Words (apart from *staycation* and *guesstimate*) are:

MOOBS Manboobs. Nobody likes this word. Mostly because nobody has used the word boobs since 1978, on *The Benny Hill Show*.

SHEEPLE Sheep-like people, i.e. the sort of lazy journalists who use words like moobs.

BLOGOSPHERE The internet equivalent of sitting in a pub full of morons all shouting at each other. This is where the sheeple go to read lots of guesstimates written by people with too much time on their hands because they're on staycation.

RECESSIONISTA One of many distant descendants of *sandinista*, a word which went from South Amercian politics via The Clash into the inane world of fashion journalism, where all language is dry-cleaned of meaning and used to sell clothes. It's just a way of trying to make saving money sound cool. Probably when they tried to call recessionistas 'people forced to cut down because they've spent all their money on stupidly over-priced rip-off "designer" clothes', it didn't go down too well.

MOST POINTLESS
PIECE OF ROYAL ETIQUETTE

According to the rules of royal etiquette one should never turn one's back on the Queen. This seems entirely unnecessary. She is very unlikely to nick anything.

THE RECORD FOR THE FASTEST EVER RANT CREATED

Is held by Marcus Brigstocke. Legend has it that Marcus read just two lines of Melanie Phillips' latest take on climate change and in just under seven seconds a fully formed twenty-minute livid repost formed itself in his head and was delivered with staggering force directly into the pages of the *Daily Mail* to the bafflement of the other passengers on the train. MB

WORST MADE-UP NICKNAME

We all know that newspapers like to use the shortest words possible in headlines; that's why people *quit* rather than resign, *wed* rather than marry and are *quizzed* rather than interviewed – and should they throw themselves off a cliff following a botched vasectomy and a messy child custody case, they will be remembered for their *heartbreak snip-op tug-of-love death-plunge horror*. But after the Scottish singer Susan Boyle became a hit on *Britain's Got Talent*, the national press decided that rather than call her 'Susan Boyle' or 'TV's Boyle', they would refer to her as SUBO.

At this point, even hardened newspaper readers flinched in horror. When the National Biscuit Company became Nabisco, it was fair enough – it was a biscuit company. When Jack Cohen bought some tea from T. E. Stockwell and became Tesco, it was fair enough – it was a trading company. But Susan Boyle is a *human being*. What these horrible coinages do is turn people into a brand for journalists to exploit; not even their name is their own any longer. They are turned, without permission, into a trademark that can be used by the press without any reference to the human being they're writing about.

They've done it with proper celebrities, inventing many ugly and stupid names including:

MADGE Madonna. The implication was that this was a genuine nickname used by the star's inner circle; it wasn't. It was just made up.

LI-LO Lindsay Lohan. As if the lezzed-up former wild child hadn't showed enough signs of a fragile personality, they thought it would be fun to send her over the edge with a demeaning nickname. One decent film might rescue her, but precious little sign of that.

BENNIFER This one sort of started it. Tabloid shorthand for Ben Affleck and Jennifer Lopez, who confusingly was already known as J-Lo, but presumably Benjlop was thought confusing.

BRANGELINA Brad Pitt and Angelina Jolie, known to their friends as 'Brad Pitt and Angelina Jolie', and known to nobody at all as Brangelina except the writers of rubbish magazines.

PHILABETH Her Majesty Queen Elizabeth II and the Prince Consort, HRH the Duke of Edinburgh.

SHELLACK Michelle and Barack Obama.

JOHUMP AND EVADAV Presenters of the *Today* programme on BBC Radio 4. It was hoped this might attract younger listeners. For the same reason, there was a high-level discussion at the BBC as to whether the *Shipping Forecast* should be renamed *Well Windy Innit?*

CLAMERON Oh stop it.

MOST HATED MILITARY EUPHEMISM

The Pentagon, and its comedy sidekick the MOD, have come up with a whole collection of coy, polysyllabic gems of PR bullshit, all designed to entice gullible journalists. Like magpies, journalists are attracted to shiny new words and rush to fill their nests with them, thereby helping the public to realise that war is not as bad as it seems. Among the favourites are:

COLLATERAL DAMAGE Blowing up buildings near the intended target and killing or maiming the innocent bystanders within them.

REDACTED Censored.

EXTRAORDINARY RENDITION Being illegally bundled onto a plane, taken to a different country and tortured, while the Brits look the other way.

FRIENDLY FIRE The absolute worst Pentagon euphemism ever. 'Friendly fire' means being killed by sharp pieces of metal ripping through your body at twice the speed of sound. The fact that they have been fired by your own army makes it worse, not better. Presumably, the top brass thought that 'friendly fire' sounded better than 'incompetent, badly trained soldiers killing their own side', since they thought that might lead to lawsuits.

The odd thing about the Pentagon is that it has such delicate, prissy euphemisms for nasty things, but tend to use nasty phrases to describe very ordinary things. For example, rather than tell a below-par soldier that he'd better buck his ideas up, US commanders will tend to say they'll 'tear him a new asshole', which is totally uncalled for. For the British, a few hours' spud-bashing will suffice.

MOST RIDICULOUS LEVEL OF OVER-EXPECTATION PLACED ON A POLITICIAN

MR B. OBAMA OF WASHINGTON If, by the time you read this, we're not all rolling in wealth, with nuclear weapons gone, global warming sorted, no leaky oil wells and everybody wandering blissfully about in a state of permanent happiness, then he's failed.

WEIRDEST THINGS OWNED BY PRINCE CHARLES

As Prince of Wales and Duke of Cornwall, Prince Charles owns rather more than the rest of us, including:

- The Oval cricket ground

- Dartmoor Prison

- The cargo of any ship wrecked off Cornwall

- The village of Daglingworth, Gloucestershire

- The estate of any Cornishman who dies without making a will

- Any whale or porpoise washed up on a Cornish beach

However, the current title-holder of Weirdest Thing is that His Royal Highness is also entitled to:

An annual tithe of 300 PUFFINS FROM THE RESIDENTS OF THE SCILLY ISLES

I bet he really insists on that last one being kept to. Once a year, he's on the phone, 'Come on, where are my puffins? I've got the pastry, I've got the onions . . .' HD

STUPIDEST FAMOUS QUOTE

The *Dictionary of Quotations* is a repository of the wittiest, wisest and most perceptive comments made through history by great writers, poets, politicians, critics, etc. It also, bizarrely, contains Margaret Thatcher's remark that 'THERE IS NO SUCH THING AS SOCIETY'.

Thatcher was never asked to explain how, if there was no such thing as society, there were organised political parties for her to become leader of; or indeed, a system of MPs representing different areas in a single meeting place called Parliament; or indeed, a governmental structure involving a law-making body, a policy-making executive, and a complex civil service system for enacting those laws; as well as a legal system for enforcing them.

It is, quite unquestionably, the most stupid remark ever made by an elected politician in a parliamentary democracy. And that's saying something.

BIGGEST LIES ON WIKIPEDIA

Wikipedia is sort of an Argos Book of Facts. It has grand designs and its heart is in the right place (although according to Wikipedia the right place for the heart is the left leg), but because it's online and is self edited by mental people, it often holds information that could fairly be described as not 100 per cent accurate. Some of this information is the result of genuine mistakes, but mostly it is put there as a sort of dissemination campaign against lazy journalists who use it as the sole source for their research. One quick glance throws up all manner of Wiki-lies that journalists have used without checking:

- The human heart tastes of peppermint. (printed as fact in *Nature Journal*, 2008)

- Ironically Van Morrison was born in a gym while Jim Morrison was born in a van. (*Smash Hits*, 1987. Journalists are so unscrupulous that this 'fact' was copied from the internet even before the internet was invented.)

- One in four potatoes is a rabbit's egg. (*Grocer's Weekly*, 2007)

- The average number of barn owls at any given wedding is four. (*Kent Weddings*, 2009)

- If you hold Enya up to your ear, you can hear the sea. (*NME*, 2005)

The best lie on Wikipedia, and thus the current record holder, is the 'fact' that Mick Hucknall is the only biological object on earth that can also be loathed from space. This isn't true, because so too can Piers Morgan.

MODERN SOCIETY, DOMESTIC

LEAST RELIABLE HOUSEHOLD ITEM

Remember your mum and dad's house? Chances are they had a cooker, and a fridge, and a toaster, and a kettle, and the chances are, they *never went wrong*. Ever. The previous generation had the same cooker, fridge, toaster, kettle, etc, for their entire lives, unless they voluntarily decided to get a newer model.

In the 21st century, however, this state of affairs simply wouldn't produce the economic growth that we like to pretend is making our lives better. Economic growth depends on buying stuff all the time and, for this reason, all household goods are now made so badly that they go wrong all the time, and need to be replaced constantly. This even includes things that *don't have anything to go wrong*, like toasters. The most expensive toaster I ever bought (a poncy Dualit retro-style one) was also the least reliable, the element failing in less than 12 months. You had to send away for a new element, which then required a midget with a fairy screwdriver to fit. I threw it away. Another poncy timer-toaster from John Lewis lasted barely 18 months. And so on and so on. I now have the cheapest, simplest toaster I could find. It makes toast.

Kettles are, if possible, worse. You would think that a kettle was the simplest object you could possibly buy, but still manufacturers have found ways to make them stop working as soon as possible. I have had kettles from several different manufacturers of varying degrees of sophistication and they were all crap. Two of them failed to switch themselves off when boiling. One switched itself off when it was nowhere near boiling. One started leaking when it was only two years old. As with toasters, the poncier they are the more rubbish they are;

the worst kettle I've owned was a moderately expensive one with a cool-looking glowing light that changed from blue to red as it boiled. The trouble was, it didn't boil. It switched itself off when the water rose above tepid. When I checked the instructions, it didn't say 'Congratulations on buying this badly made, shit kettle that doesn't work but has a cool-looking light in it!' It didn't say that. And it should have done. (See SUBJECTS MOST LIKELY TO TURN ME INTO JEREMY CLARKSON.)

Kettles and toasters and fridges are, of course, electrical items – we haven't even started on *electronic* items yet, and they're even worse. Go to any recycling centre in Britain and you will always see a pile of portable radio-CD players that look almost new; this is because they *are* almost new, and have already gone wrong. The average CD tray lasts about six months. Less if it's a flip-up. If you look in your larder, you'll find jars of pasta sauce that have lasted longer than the average CD player.

The acknowledged current record holder in this category, however, is the TV DIGIBOX. Early models were hurriedly bashed together in a large shed somewhere to cash in on Freeview, and were quite simply the least reliable consumer item ever built. It was quite common to spend over £100 on one only to find it stopped working after a couple of months. (I know, because I checked the internet message boards, which were full of other suckers howling into the ether about their rubbish digiboxes.) Nobody cared, or even noticed. Pictures froze, recordings jammed, channels vanished – no one gave a toss. As so often in modern consumer society, you are abandoned after purchase to an endless purgatory of premium-rate helplines and web-based troubleshooting FAQs. This is the wondrous free-market economy that has done so jolly well recently.

MOST POINTLESS ELECTRICAL RETAILER'S SO-CALLED GOLD WARRANTY

The record for this goes to a kettle costing £6.99 on offer in the Nuneaton branch of a certain High Street electrical retail outlet in Warwickshire, UK, in 2002. It was sold by an opportunist Saturday boy who bamboozled a confused old lady into taking out extra cover for three years at the exorbitant cost of £68 per year. Thus, the total gross cost of the £6.99 kettle that day was calculated at £210.99 or, in layman's terms, 'a rip-off'. The kettle itself broke within a week, but couldn't be replaced or repaired because the confused old lady in question was Jon's mental octogenarian nana who had admittedly broken the terms of the warranty the moment she immersed the whole thing in a pan of boiling water whilst trying to cook an unopened tin of baked beans in it. The resulting repairs to the fire-damaged kitchen were estimated at £8,000 by the insurance company, meaning that in the end the actual total cost of the kettle was somewhere in the region of £8,210.99. JH

TEN MOST STUPIDLY NAMED ITEMS OF IKEA FURNITURE

10 Møømintrøll (chest of drawers)

9 Scøøby Døø (fitted kitchen)

8 Pal Waakatar (cutlery)

7 Ragnørøk (apocalyptic shoe organiser)

6 Jøey Tempest (lead singer with the band Europe)

5 M. Night Shyamalan (lamp. Burned brightly initially, but not now)

4 Schnørbitz (CD and DVD storage solution)

3 Tøwnsend Thørensøn (wardrobe. Doors don't close properly)

2 Beøwulf (long, complicated bookcase)

1 Skøl (gassy, unpleasant tasting sofa range brewed in a fjord)

MOST-BODGED DIY JOBS (OUTDOOR)

PRUNING is a tedious job that has to be done once a year, in spring or autumn; the DIY gardener will just guess which. This will stunt and/or kill the plant in question, saving you the bother of having to prune it again.

PLANTING is the process of taking a healthy plant from a garden centre, removing it from its pot, and putting it in the ground. Once in the ground, a combination of slugs, snails, cats, foxes, birds, greenfly, blackfly and leaf-rot will reduce it to a stump within two to three weeks. The only way to stop this happening is to tend it constantly, surrounding it with eggshells, coffee-grounds, slug pellets, netting and land-mines. Nobody under the age of 65 has time to do this, which is why only retired people are really good at gardening.

MOWING is a man's job, done on a Sunday morning either before or after washing the car. It is relatively simple but, depending on the number of children's toys/barbecue cutlery/ pebbles hidden in the lawn, it can be costly in new blades. The world's most dangerous mower is an electric Flymo, which in running over its own power-cord adds the risk of electrocution to the risk of dismemberment. Sunday morning is probably the most hazardous few hours of the week.

FENCING Certain jobs should be tackled only by a professional, and fencing is one of them. Many a suburban householder has underestimated the danger of trying to put up a fence yourself. It looks easy, but the problem is that when the wind gets up, a garden fence becomes an offensive weapon. A six-foot wooden pole, falling in the right direction, can cause more damage than Millwall's away fans on a bad day. After any gale-force wind in Britain, the suburbs are littered with bits of fence, damaged cars and squashed cats. Somewhere under the wreckage will be a bloke going, 'Oh – that's what those big metal spikes were for.'

BIGGEST SIGN OF
LOSS OF YOUTH

There are many indications that you finally have to accept
Grown-Up status. They generally occur in our late twenties or
early thirties and often include the following symptoms:

- Not caring what's Number 1 in the charts

- A growing wish that you'd like to find a milkman

- A creeping tendency to notice that the boring town you
  grew up in and used to hate, actually has some rather
  nice houses (depending on the road, obviously)

However, the world record in this category is held by MR STEVE
PUNT, who when asked by his parents what he wanted for his
28th birthday, replied that what he'd really like was one of those
carving trays with spikes on so you can carve a Sunday joint
without it sliding all over the place.* The realisation that this
mundane, yet practical, necessity was his greatest current desire
caused a temporary feeling of despair and depression. Although
frankly, a nice bit of roast lamb soon sorted that out.

Another strong contender in this category is Jon Holmes, who
once found himself standing in a supermarket genuinely unable
to decide between sun-dried or sun-blushed tomatoes.

---

*In other words, a very useful thing. But see also WEDDING-LIST ITEM,
MOST POINTLESS

MOST INCOMPREHENSIBLE THING TO MEN

WOMEN

MOST POINTLESS ADVERTISING BOAST

The world's most pointless advert boasting is by a certain brand of household toilet cleaner, which for many years has proudly proclaimed that it 'KILLS 99% OF ALL KNOWN GERMS'. It says this as if killing 99% of all known germs is a good thing for your toilet.

The success of this slogan indicates how, more than 150 years after *The Origin of Species*, Darwin's theory is still very poorly understood. If the bleach in question kills 99% of the germs, that means the 1% that survive are bleach-resistant. They will, therefore, *breed bleach-resistant offspring* and the next time you spray cleaner down your bog, a much higher proportion of germs will survive, because there will be a higher proportion of resistant ones than last time. Every time you clean your loo, you are killing off the susceptible ones while the resistant ones multiply unchecked. Eventually your crapper is crawling with resistant bacteria and your bog-cleaner can do *nothing about it*.

This makes the slogan quite poor and deeply misleading. Really, the advert ought to end like this:

**FIRM MALE VOICE: Kills 99% of all known germs . . . (pause)
the first time you use it. And then a steadily diminishing
percentage of the total germs as natural selection allows the
survivors to breed.**

But that, frankly, isn't quite as catchy. (And also, incidentally,
explains why Richard Dawkins is never asked to do commercials.)

We also haven't even begun to consider the implications of the
word 'known'. If something kills 99% of all known germs, that's
an acknowledgement that there may be other, unknown germs
of which the bleach-makers know nothing. Again, the phrasing
is very careful to avoid its real meaning, which would be an
advert that went:

**FIRM MALE VOICE: Kills 99% of all known germs, leaving
only the mutant strains unknown to science, and the resistant
ones that are going to take over your toilet.**

And if that was the slogan, they wouldn't sell much bleach.

I urge you, before you set out to buy any bathroom hygiene
products, to put on your shopping list: 'Be sure to consider the
operation of natural selection in the production of immune
bacteria.' The NHS didn't, and we ended up with MRSA. Which,
ironically, kills 99% of all known patients.

MOST ANNOYING FACET OF SERVICE CULTURE

'Service culture' is a business buzzword which means constantly talking about service rather than actually giving you any, and its nadir is the **CUSTOMER SATISFACTION SURVEY**.

It is obviously a good thing that companies try to stay closer to the needs and wants of their customers – it makes the whole process of buying and selling goods and services much more efficient and better targeted. However, in spite of this emphasis on customer 'wants', no one yet seems to have realised that the one thing customers really don't want is to be *constantly asked what they thought of the service* with which they have just been provided. Customers hate customer satisfaction surveys, but every single organisation sends you them.

In the old days when my car was serviced I would pick it up at the end of the day, pay the man, and that would be that. Now, four or five days after the service I get a letter through the post checking that I was happy with the work done and asking me to 'rate the experience', by filling in the small card they have sent me. Was I **dissatisfied/ satisfied/delighted** or **highly delighted** with the manner in which the work was done? Was I **unimpressed/impressed/highly impressed** with the attitude of the staff? Would I agree **weakly/ strongly/very strongly/ really really really massively strongly** that the level of service delivered would lead me to visit the showroom again? And so on through ten meaningless categories. So I don't fill it in, and consign it to the recycling.

Unfortunately this is not enough to shake them off my trail. So two weeks later, when it has become obvious to the dealer that their form has now gone to serve a greater purpose, and is perhaps by now re-incarnated as a copy of the *Daily Star*, or a roll of Andrex, they phone me up. Fortunately I am out and it goes to ansaphone. They are just phoning to check that I am happy with the service I have received and would I mind giving them a quick call to let them know. **Aaaaargh**, could they not read the sub-text of 'the card not being sent back'? I ignore it once again. All is fine for a few days and then there is another call in response to the fact that I haven't called, and this time I make the mistake of answering the phone. They are worried. Is the fact that I haven't called perhaps because I was dissatisfied with the service? Does it mean that perhaps I might agree strongly with the statement 'I would not visit the dealership again'?

No, I try to explain, it doesn't mean any of those things. What it means is that **no one in their right mind could be 'highly delighted' with the servicing of their car**. Servicing a car is really expensive and inconvenient and leaves you without a car for a day, none of which is delightful. No one cares about the ambience of the showroom, or wants to suggest ways in which the layout of the greeting area might be improved. No one wants to rate the quality of the beverages on offer or the cleanliness of the toilet facilities. It's not Starbucks, for God's sake – a cup of lukewarm Clix stuff is fine as long as they **service your car while you drink it**. Had I been dissatisfied with the service received, like I'd just left the garage and a door had fallen off, I would have let them know. Surely that is good enough for them? Believe me, the last thing any of us want is to be stalked by a needy car dealer wanting to know how our relationship is going. So next time, to stop it getting out of hand – I really don't want a boiled bunny in my radiator – I am going to hand over the keys and a restraining order.

HOW HAVE YOU ENJOYED THIS ENTRY IN THE NOW SHOW BOOK?

Please tick the appropriate box.

☐ Not a lot
☐ Quite a lot
☐ A lot
☐ More than a lot
☐ Goodness me, hugely

I would read this entry again. Do you agree with this statement?

☐ Slightly
☐ Strongly
☐ Very Strongly
☐ Sorry, can't stop I'm reading the entry again

How cross does it make you when you get one of these surveys?

☐ Really cross
☐ Psychotically cross
☐ F*** off. F*** off the lot of you.
☐ Stop now, I've got a knife

MOST POINTLESS WEDDING-LIST ITEM

Fish Kettle

MOST STRESSFUL SPECIAL OCCASION

The most stressful special occasions in the calendar are WEDDING ANNIVERSARIES. With most yearly occasions (birthdays, etc.) one merely has to remember the date; with wedding anniversaries one has to know the date of the anniversary, *which* anniversary it is and *what* commemorative element or substance pertains to this particular anniversary.

While some of these commemorative elements and substances are well known (silver for 25th anniversary, gold for 50th and so on) some are much more obscure and hard to remember. The full list is as follows:

1st   –   Paper

2nd   –   Cotton

3rd   –   Leather

4th   –   PVC

5th   –   Wood

6th   –   Linoleum

7th   –   MDF

8th   –   Bronze

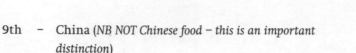

9th – China (*NB NOT Chinese food – this is an important distinction*)

10th – Tin

11th – Steel

12th – Polyester mix

13th – Phlegm

14th – Amnesia

15th – String

16th – Cheese

17th – Ammonia

18th – TBC

19th – Ennui

20th – China again (*in case you made a fool of yourself with egg fried rice 11 years ago*)

21st – Tarmac

22nd – Bacon

23rd – Glue

24th – Spandex

25th – Silver

26th – There isn't one

27th – No, really, baby, there isn't one, they start again at 30th

28th – Honey, are we gonna have this conversation every year?

29th – Guess so (sigh)

30th – There! Pearl! 30th is Pearl! You happy now?

35th – Cubic Zirconium

40th – Vindaloo

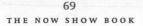

45th – Kevlar

50th – Gold

60th – Diamond

70th – Plutonium

80th – Kryptonite

90th – Dilithium Crystal

The most technically problematic of these is the 14th anniversary, the Amnesia Anniversary (one of only two anniversaries to be commemorated by an abstract concept; the other being Ennui, which is . . . oh, who cares). In order to remember it, one has to forget it, and it can be very difficult to convince one's spouse that you did actually remember to forget it, rather than simply forgetting it. Before the 1970s, Plutonium pertained to the 45th anniversary, but was relegated out of harm's way to the 70th after Herschel Liebowitz of Middletown, Pennsylvania, accidentally triggered the Three Mile Island incident while trying to pick up a late anniversary gift for his parents.

MOST ANNOYING
RECORDED ANNOUNCEMENT

This is, by definition, a difficult category as all recorded announcements, be they on the train (see TRAIN ANNOUNCEMENTS, LEAST EXPLICABLE), technical support helpline, tube ('Mind the GAP, Mind the GAP'), aeroplane, supermarket or that scary one that we'll get in the instance of a nuclear war that Frankie Goes to Hollywood nicked in the 1980s for their song 'Two Tribes'. But to find the most annoying one, let us consider the supermarket.

What we're dealing with here is the voice of the self-service automated checkout machine that has crept into supermarkets over the last few years with the specific intention of driving shoppers mental. And the single most irksome thing about self-service checkout machines is the sonorous voice that there is an 'unexpected item in the bagging area'.

The main reason that this is so infuriating is that, by definition, anything that one places in the aforementioned bagging area has more than likely come from the shelves of the very supermarket that you are in: a tin of dog food, say, or a box of cornflakes or a radish. Granted, if one were to place in the bagging area say an owl, or a gun, or a tractor, or a coelacanth, or even if one were to pull down one's trousers, squat over the bagging area to demonstrate directly into it exactly what one thinks of this stupid announcement, then, yes, the machine might have a point. So, if by chance any self-service checkout machines are reading this (it's possible, after all they can't read barcodes properly so they must be busy reading something else) kindly allow me, at the risk of repeating myself, to tell you once and for all that if I give you a jar of coffee or a can of Carlsberg to price up and scan, this should not come as a surprise to you. Just shut your electric mouth and do your job. I only wish to hear your unexpected item announcement if I astonish you with something you certainly aren't expecting, such as, for example, a judge's wig or an egret or a severed head. If I was to place one of these items in your bagging area then I would have no problem at all with you choosing to speak up. As I haven't, you shouldn't, yet you still do and this is insanely irritating.

Of course, I actually think it might be just me that these machines don't like. Last week I walked past a rival, posher, more expensive supermarket and through the window I saw one

MP putting a tennis court through the machine and another scanning a mock-Tudor moat and neither of them seemed to be having any trouble. That's the problem – it's one rule for them and another for us, isn't it?

'Unexpected item in the bagging area' is probably the most annoying recorded announcement in the world. (See MOST UNEXPECTED ITEM IN THE BAGGING AREA.) JH

BIGGEST MISCONCEPTION ABOUT MEN

There are many clichés about men that are lazy rubbish 'Men are frightened of commitment' is one – this is basically just a way of saying 'alack, for no man hath asked me to marry!' without sounding old-fashioned.

The biggest misconceptions about men, however, concern their standards of hygiene. According to the advertising industry, no male can operate a washing machine (see MOST TEDIOUS TV COMMERCIAL CLICHÉ) and **men can go for up to three years without changing their pants**. Furthermore, it is frequently alleged that men rely on their wives or girlfriends to do their ironing for them.

This is simply not true. According to market research, 17 per cent of men do their own ironing – on one condition. Namely, that they can go out and buy a Man's Iron. Not some pastel-coloured girlie iron which squirts decorous little puffs of steam like some sort of mechanical cologne dispenser – no, men want a fearsome off-road iron, the sort of iron Jeremy Clarkson might use on his jeans. It's entirely possible that you think I'm joking, but no. According to the research, men are the *most profitable* iron-buying customers because they insist on the most expensive gadget-ridden models. Women just want to get the creases out of their clothes – men want to *destroy* them. This kind of thing was, of course, pioneered by the shaving industry, with all that stuff about a 'first blade that shaves you close, then a second blade that shaves you closer still, and then a third blade that burns off any remaining stubble with a flamethrower, and then a fourth blade that sands the skin down prior to applying two coats of Dulux Weathershield', etc etc. Does this tactic now apply to all household goods? 'Women just want a fridge to keep things cold. Men want to reduce the temperature of food to absolute zero so the molecules cease moving. Only then is the beer ready to drink.'

DATES MOST LIKELY TO FEATURE IN A HISTORY EXAM

1066 The Norman Conquest

1215 Signing of the Magna Carta

1349 The Black Death

1666 The Great Fire of London

1805 The Battle of Trafalgar

1815 The Battle of Waterloo

1914 Start Of WW1

1936 Abdication Crisis

1945 End of WW2

1969 First Moon Landing

2008 World Economic Collapse

2010 Britain comes last in Eurovision Song Contest

2012 Ancient Mayan Calendar proves accurate and world ends, thus removing all worries about the London Olympic legacy.

MOST UNEXPECTED ITEM IN THE BAGGING AREA

The record for the Most Unexpected Item In The Bagging Area is held by me when I placed in it a large, heavy, earth-filled ornamental concrete flower tub from the car park, just to see what would happen. What happened was that I was thrown out of the shop. To add insult to injury, even though there was now a completely unexpected soil-crammed concrete pot in its bagging area, the machine didn't say a word, largely because it was now broken. JH

RUDEST NAME FOR A RACEHORSE

Horse-racing authorities throughout the world devote much time to stopping owners giving their horses names which sound rude, especially when read fast during race commentaries. For this reason the Jockey Club, which administers the sport in Britain, has barred the names *Far Canal* and *Hoof Hearted*, although *Wear the Fox Hat*, *Noble Locks*, *Joe Blob* and *Mary Hinge* have all raced in Britain. The system abroad is equally stringent. The French horse-racing authorities recently refused to register a horse called *Gros Nichons* and for good reason, the name isn't even a play on words, colloquially it means 'big tits'. Well done the French authorities, except that the owners then thought for a while about what they would now like to call their horse, and re-submitted it. The authorities registered it without a murmur under its new name, and *BIG TITS* duly took to the track.

LEAST IMAGINATIVE WISH

Asked for their ultimate ambition, the thing they would most like to do before they die, most people's imagination seizes up and they grope for clichés of staggering banality. Statistically, the most common ultimate dream is to SWIM WITH DOLPHINS. Far from being an unobtainable fantasy, this is widely available at many classy Florida establishments along with English breakfasts and weddings with thrones.

Why, for the love of Flipper, would anyone dream of swimming with dolphins? You can't keep up with them, they will show you up by jumping through hoops and walking on their tails and then going 'Now you do that, smartarse' and, worst of all, they will ask you awkward questions about why the Japanese eat them.

Of course, turns out most people who say they want to 'swim with dolphins' don't want to do any such thing – what they actually want to do is 'grab hold of a dolphin's dorsal fin and then get dragged along by it'. This isn't swimming. This is just getting dragged through the water by a dolphin, which is dubious in moral terms and pointless in terms of cardio-vascular exercise.

Interestingly, when dolphins are asked about their ultimate ambitions, over 78 per cent say that it is to 'avoid being used as a lifestyle accessory by idiots'.

(See THE TEN THINGS YOU SHOULD MAKE THE LEAST EFFORT TO DO BEFORE YOU DIE.)

MOST LUDICROUS GOVERNMENT PUBLICATION

The Department for Environment, Food and Rural Affairs has recently published their DRAFT CONSULTATION CODE OF PRACTICE FOR THE WELFARE OF CATS, a document for cat owners telling them how to feed their animals, where they should go to the toilet and including details on sleeping arrangements and the need for pet privacy. It is thought to be the first in a series of Codes of Practice for all domesticated pets. Guinea pig owners will, of course, be able to provide both sleeping arrangements and privacy by shredding the pamphlet and using it to line the hutch.

For cats, the pamphlet is 28 pages long; 28 pages telling you what you can and can't do with a cat; 28 pages telling you what you must do when looking after an animal that takes no notice of anything you say; 28 pages telling you how to make it easier for the cat to do precisely what it likes. Can you imagine a cat's reaction to us giving them a code of conduct?

Conduct points

One: If a human calls, you must come.
Cat response: Piss off.

Two: No furballs on the carpet.
Cat response: Hang on, hang on, there's one coming.

Three: Don't pull threads from the sofa.
Cat response: Ha, ha.

Four: You must eat everything on your plate.
Cat response: I'm going next door now.

Five: Only jump on your owner's lap when asked.
Cat response: Who writes this stuff?

You see, it is a one-sided arrangement, and if they won't accept a code of conduct why the hell should we? Of course we should look after our pets, but is a code of conduct really the way to go? It wouldn't happen in any other country in the world. The French, for example, would find it laughable, and for them it isn't just pets. It's all sorts of animals:

'Where is Toad?' said Ratty.

'He's here', said Moley, 'but I'm not sure coming to France was a very good idea. He has had an accident. He was caught this morning by gastronomes.'

'Where are his legs?' said Ratty.

'Gone, I'm afraid', said Toad. 'But look on the bright side. Now I'll be able to get a disabled parking space.'

MOST ARGUED-OVER BOARD GAME

Monopoly is arguably the most famous of all board games, if you don't count chess. And Monopoly provokes far more arguments. Especially among the British, where the game continues to fascinate a nation that, perhaps more than any in the world, has a fetish for property ownership. No other country in the world has quite Britain's love for buying houses, doing them up, selling them, renting them, watching TV shows about them, reading the books of the TV shows about them, taking out the mortgage to buy the house to do like they did in the book of the TV show about them and getting very very cross that they can't borrow the money so easily any more.

Of course, Monopoly has always been popular around the world. Even in Soviet Russia there was a version, but it was admittedly very dull. You went round the board landing on streets and railway stations, and you couldn't buy any of them because they were all the property of the State and the Russian people. Every now and then you would pick up a Chance card and it would say, 'You have been overheard questioning the accuracy of the statistics on coal production. Go straight to

Siberia.' However, the break-up of the Soviet Union led to a big new market and a popular, new version of the game in which players would land on a railway station and find that the whole railway system had been given to them free in exchange for political loyalty. Immensely popular in the early 1990s, copies of this version of the game are now sought after, particularly for the Chance card which reads: 'Boris Yeltsin has given you the entire aluminium industry. Go and buy a football team.'

Monopoly is a very adaptable game, which is one reason for its enduring popularity. The legendary 1980s version can allegedly still be found on eBay, in which the waterworks and railway stations are sold off far too cheaply and the player elected as Banker has to wear a striped shirt with a white collar or be disqualified. There is a large pile of Chance cards, but all the Community Chest cards simply read: 'There is no such thing as community.' In the end, the owner of a house in the Old Kent Road is asked to pay the same poll tax as the owner of a hotel on Mayfair, the board is overturned and set on fire. The game was abandoned in 1990, although many people are still nostalgic for it even now. David Cameron has promised to bring some of it back, but only the bits people liked.

Monopoly has, though, failed to really capitalise on the recent economic collapse. A truly modern version would allow players to buy a house in Mayfair, turn it into buy-to-let flats in the hope of making a killing out of younger people priced out of the market – and then find it has dropped in value and they can't sell it. At this point, all the other players must point at them and laugh, shouting 'serves you right, you greedy arse' and evict them from the game.

There is also the controversial question of being sent to jail. In a modern version, any player sent directly to jail and not allowed to collect their £200 should be allowed to sell their story to a

Sunday newspaper afterwards, earning up to £150,000 in the process. This would, however, mean one player agreeing to act as Max Clifford. Many people may refuse to do this, on grounds of conscience.

LEAST SUCCESSFUL AND MOST UNAPPEALING PARTWORK MAGAZINE

Every January, as Christmas flops exhaustedly from view and your New Year's resolutions are already a distant memory (see *RESOLUTION, MOST QUICKLY BROKEN NEW YEAR'S*), it is impossible not to notice the sudden proliferation of television adverts for so-called partwork magazines, the kind that encourage you to 'build your collection week by week until they eventually fill up a forgotten corner of the garage. Issue one comes with a free binder'.

These hateful wastes of paper spend January of every year prostituting their wares but, without fail, each one is guaranteed to have disappeared from the newsagent's shelves within a month. Who knows why they appear at this time of year? It's become an annual event like bird migration, the trooping of the salmon or Boy George being arrested for something. And where do they go? Presumably, come the onset of March they swim back upstream to their publishers to die, ready to re-spawn the very next year. And they normally vanish round about the time of issue three when you're the proud owner of two now-useless bolts and one plastic wheel towards your build-it-yourself remote-controlled car. Every single one of

.... ⌐∂ ....

these magazines disappears faster than an armed Met Officer's notes into the shooting of an unarmed Brazilian, but some go quicker than others. Contenders for the least successful and most unappealing partwork magazine are as follows:

HOME OCEAN BUILDER Week by week, drop by drop, transform your home into an ocean! Part one comes with a free sachet of salt water to start your collection!

CONTAMINATED NEEDLECRAFT Month by month builds into a rewarding hobby for intravenous drug users!

COLLECT EVERY EPISODE OF *ONLY FOOLS AND HORSES* **EVER MADE FOR SOME SAD REASON!** Part one comes with advice on the best way to kill yourself and end your worthless, empty life.

HANDY WICKER MAN BUILDER The handy step-by-step guide to constructing my own 60-foot-high wicker man on a remote Scottish island! Learn how to lure a policeman inside and then burn it to bits with this handy all-colour guide to sacrifice! Part one comes with a free bit of wicker and a match to get you started.

THE A–Z OF GREAT BRITISH RACISTS Issue two: Davidson to Griffin.

THE COMPLETE WARPLANE FANCIER A fortnightly compendium for anyone who is sexually aroused by warplanes.

Come January, all of these magazines try to tempt you. They're like the glossy publishing equivalent of Jesus in the desert being propositioned by Satan.

'Come on', says Satan, 'you know you've always wanted to own every edition of *Little House on the Prairie* on DVD. And even if you haven't, what have you got to lose? Look, each one comes with a full-colour comprehensive guide to all of the characters in an accompanying magazine. Come on, you know you want to. It's only £1.99. What's £1.99 for a lifetime of unbridled Prairie-based TV nostalgia? Come on . . .'

So you buy it. But then Satan's going 'Hahahaha! Got you, you snivelling vacant shell of a human being! The first one may well have been £1.99, but the next issues are *£1,000 each*!! Hahahahaaa. And we will be gone by March. Loser.'

I have a confession to make. When I was younger I collected a partwork called *The Unexplained* which claimed to examine UFOs, ghosts and the paranormal but failed to shed any light on why, after issue five, the whole thing mysteriously vanished, leaving me *a) none the wiser about Bigfoot and b) the disappointed owner of a two-thirds empty free binder.*

And that's the other thing. There's always a free binder. What we need is a magazine that gives away a free binder that will bind together all of the useless free binders: *Part Work Binder Collector* – a sort of monthly partwork binder collector that comes with a free binder in which to neatly sort all the useless half empty free binders that the avid partwork collector accumulates each year. Trouble is, issue one would just come with a free label or something so you'd be encouraged to build your binder over 12 issues and then by March it'd be gone, leaving you with only half a binder-binder with which to bind your binders and then you'd simply be back to square one.

Anyway, the world record for the least appealing partwork magazine goes to the forthcoming *THE COMPLETE JADE MODELLER*. 'Week by week, step by step, build your own working model of Brave Jade™. Ever wanted to be a famous publicist? Well, now's your chance, as once complete, the Tragic Bermondsey Princess™ Doll can be manipulated and positioned to your own ends, just like the real thing.' JH

WORLD'S MOST HYSTERIA-LADEN HEALTH WARNINGS

The world's most hysterical health warnings are those on BRITISH CIGARETTE PACKETS. These began in 1971 as the simple:

Warning. Cigarettes can damage your health

Since then, the tone of the messages has been one of rising hysteria. In 1991 the warning became:

Cigarettes can seriously damage your health

In 1994:

Smoking Kills

To be swiftly followed by:

Smoking can cause a long and painful death

And most recently:

Smoke contains benzene, nitrosamines, formaldehyde and hydrogen cyanide

With pictures next to it showing quite how horrible the effects of smoking can be.

Yet, in spite of the fact that the arguments against smoking are so clear cut and that, logically, people should just stop doing it, the warnings have gone largely unheeded and people have carried on puffing away. This may be partially down to the fact that they sound like the kind of thing your parents might say to stop you doing something, and since when did that ever work? In fact, the kind of things parents actually would say might have been more effective, as parents have the freedom to make up their own scientific evidence.

Smoking – Don't or you'll turn into a cigarette, you will

Smoking – Don't get cross, but it makes you less intelligent. I'm just saying

Smoking – The effects last for years, it makes you really ugly and your bits might fall off

They might have worked. Or perhaps they should have tried the old parental tactic of reverse psychology, with warnings like:

Smoking – Go on. We want you to smoke

Smoking – We're on 60 a day down at the Department of Health

Hysteria, however, simply doesn't work, which if they thought about it, the government already know. After all, they don't use the technique for any other kind of signage. Road signs, for example, simply say 'Dangerous Bend Ahead'. They don't say 'Dangerous Bend Ahead. Yes, Coming Up! Look Out! You're going too fast. Too fast, I tell you!' Electricity sub-stations have a very simple sign saying 'Danger of Death' and a line drawing of a dead man to reinforce the point. They don't say 'Don't Come in Here! Danger of Death! Danger of Really Nasty Death! Don't Touch Anything! Run!'

This is because, at heart, the government know that the best way to get us to do anything is to tell us simply, clearly and calmly what might happen, which in the case of cigarettes is this. *You might die!*

Oh no, now I've fallen into their trap.

LONGEST WAIT FOR BT TO COME ROUND AND INSTALL BROADBAND AFTER ORDERING

In February 2006, Cliff Peters, 37, a recruitment consultant of Bedford, UK, ordered British Telecom's Option 2 broadband package via the telephone at an installation cost of £88.09 + VAT and £20 per month thereafter. At first, all seemed well as he was told an engineer would arrive within five working days. After six working days nothing had happened, so Mr Peters called the BT Broadband helpline. After being on hold for a week, he eventually got through to an automated voice which gave him 16 options and then cut him off. Angry, he called a different number, which had a person on it. This person apologised and claimed the original order had been lost, despite the money having gone out of Mr Peters's account. Assurances were given that broadband would be up and running in Mr Peters's house the next day. Two days later, Mr Peters called BT again. This time he spoke to a different person, but because he had forgotten to get the name of the original person he had to start all over again. Assurances were given that broadband would be up and running in Mr Peters's house the next day. The next day was a Saturday. The following Tuesday, Mr Peters called again to enquire why 'the f*ck', when he still had no broadband, were 'you ar*eholes' already taking a monthly direct debit for it out of his account? By the following Friday, Mr Peters had decided life was too short, and simply gave up. A month later, an engineer arrived while he was out and connected an unwanted Freeview box to his neighbour's house. This to-ing and fro-ing went on for three years. In July 2009, Mr Peters called BT for the 922nd time to complain again. At the time of writing, he is still on hold.

MOST ANNOYING THINGS

An actual survey carried out a couple of years ago came to the conclusion that the most annoying thing in modern Britain is COLD-CALLERS. They worked this out by cold-calling people and asking them if they'd take part in a survey, so you'd have to say the sample may have been skewed.

Selected highlights of the survey results were as follows:

2 **Caravans** This seems a bit harsh. I mean, they're a bit annoying if you're stuck behind one on a single-carriageway road but, to be honest, how often does that happen?

3 **Queue jumpers** Everyone hates queue jumpers, but people seldom confront them. When they do, they don't take any notice because, often, they're foreign. Foreigners don't understand queueing. Neither do old people, who always assume that they can barge to the front of a bus queue on the grounds that they have been alive longer than everyone else.

4 **James Blunt** Ah, the fickle finger of fashion. James Blunt would still love to be that unpopular.

5 **Traffic wardens** In what way are traffic wardens annoying? They're there to stop lazy, self-righteous drivers jamming everyone else, by parking in the wrong place. They're just doing their job. Leave them alone. Apart from the one that ticketed me in my own road, the officious bastard.

9 **Ex-smokers** Fair enough, but ex-smokers are nowhere near as annoying as vegetarians, who aren't on the list at all. (Not all vegetarians, just the ones who pass comments on other people's food in public. They should have been top five.)

11 **Hangovers** 'Annoying' is not really the right word here. 'Liable to induce temporary bout of self-loathing and short-lived promise to go teetotal which collapses within days' is nearer the mark.

12 **Carol Vorderman** Poor old Carol – what's she done to deserve that? Apart from advertising loans while simultaneously making a packet teaching maths?

13 **Loud mobile users** Obviously. Everyone hates them. But, on the other hand, where would stand-up comics be without them?

14 **Men in flip-flops** Seems a bit harsh. And sexist. Besides, men in Crocs are far worse. The red ones make them look like Sonic the Hedgehog on a day out.

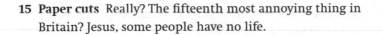

15 Paper cuts Really? The fifteenth most annoying thing in Britain? Jesus, some people have no life.

19 Off milk Ooooh. Sounds all right to me.

20 Being put on hold It's not so much being put on hold that's annoying, as being told every ten seconds that you are still on hold. That's the difference between something being a bit annoying, and something causing a psychotic outburst and a spate of frenzied killings.

21 Motorcyclists who weave through traffic

And

22 Drivers who park in disabled bays Right. And yet at number 5 – traffic wardens. So the people who break the law *are less annoying than the people who try and stop them doing it. Stupid survey.*

100 Pointless surveys I made that up.

DATES LEAST LIKELY TO FEATURE IN A HISTORY EXAM

1067 – William had Conquered, there was little resistance to Norman control, and even our French conquerors were behaving themselves; no angry farmers had blockaded Thanet, Rye or any of the Channel ports and the only lamb being burned was by English peasants not yet used to cooking it pink, inserting slivers of garlic and sprinkling it with sprigs of rosemary.

The only excitement was that work began on the Tower of London, the Norman fortress in the heart of the capital. The design was Norman, the builders must have been British. It was finished in 1532.

1216 – Nothing happened. King John very bored, wandering round his castle muttering, 'This time last year at least I had the signing of the Magna Carta to look forward to.'

1348 – All very quiet. Health officials very pleased by the low mortality rate. Even the *Daily Mail* was fairly content, save for the odd article about the numbers of Lombard plumbers in London, Flemish Weavers stealing British jobs, and a scaremongering story about a plague approaching from the continent.

1667 – Historically insignificant, and little is known about it save for the year's most asked question: 'Can you smell burning again?'

1806 – Very quiet year, particularly for Nelson.

1816   Waterloo now a fading memory, except among a group of transport executives who think it might be the best of the various names they have brainstormed for a new railway terminus, ever hopeful that by recalling our greatest ever victory over the French it might make commuters less pissed off that French trains are more reliable, more comfortable, half the price and twice the speed of our own.

1913 – All Quiet on Every Front

1935 – No wars anywhere. Prince Edward scared that his father may soon die, and he may be required to become king, hence the phrase 'Coronation Chicken'.

1946 – Lots of international meetings about how to make Europe homely again. No one notices the Russians measuring the continent for curtains.

1968 – Neil Armstrong wonders if he would rather go on Apollo 11 and be the first man on the moon, or wait until Apollo 13 and be the star of a Hollywood movie.

2007 – Everything is hunky dory, particularly in the banking sector.

TELEVISION
AND
RADIO

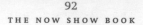

BIGGEST
BBC FAKE UNCOVERED
DURING NOTORIOUS
BBC FAKERY SCANDAL

In 2008, a high-level Ofcom investigation found former *The One Show* presenter Adrian Chiles to not be real.

MOST CLICHÉD
TV DOCUMENTARY

Only a small handful of subjects are considered suitable for TV documentaries. They are the pyramids, the Titanic, and anything to do with Hitler. If you can work in the royals too, so much the better. The dream of every TV executive is to be able to commission a programme called *RAISE THE SPHINX: HOW PRINCESS DIANA WAS MURDERED TO PROTECT THE SECRET OF HITLER'S QUEST TO RECOVER THE LOST TREASURE OF THE PHARAOHS OFF THE ATLANTIC FLOOR.*

Oldeft sitcom
(OLDEST SITCOM)

Last Of The Summer Wine dates from the early medieval period, when it was part of the York Mystery Plays, under the title *Ye Sumer Wine Is Icumen In*. There was an Elizabethan comedy,

A *Midsummer-Night's Wine*, which was performed at the Globe
Theatre in 1599, and is believed to have influenced Shakespeare
to avoid Yorkshire for the rest of his life. The text is lost and we
only know of the play's existence from a mention in a letter by a
contemporary traveller, who describes it as 'the amusinge trialls
of three Olde Bloakes in the Northern Country'.

The Restoration comedy *The Pensioner's Revenge*, or, *Downhill in a
Bath-Tub*, was premiered at Drury Lane in 1683. The amusing saga
was revived constantly throughout the 18th and 19th centuries,
inspiring Ibsen's only Yorkshire-set play, *Nora Batty*, described as
'Hedda Gabler with latts'.

The show first appeared on radio in 1922, the same week
the BBC opened. Under the strict rules of John Reith, the first
Director-General, it was decided that Yorkshire accents were not
allowed, so the setting was re-located to Berkshire. References to
alcohol were also strictly forbidden, so up until 1938 the show
ran under the title *Last of the Elderflower Tonic*. In the 1950s these
rules were relaxed, and work began on developing a TV version.
The rest, as they say, is history.

MOST IMITABLE
FICTIONAL TV DOG

This depends on who you are. For instance, if you are Mitch Benn
then the answer is either SCOOBY DOO (one must bellow a cry
of 'Yaggy!') or if you are Steve Punt then it is MUTTLEY from *The
Wacky Races* (a sort of hissing laugh every time Dick Dastardly
fails to catch the pigeon). If you are Jon Holmes then the most
imitable fictional TV dog is CHURCHILL from the Churchill car

insurance adverts (a sort of droll northern doggy brogue). A typical impression of Churchill might work like this (it helps to picture the dog):

STEVE PUNT: Jon, can you do an impression of Scooby Doo, or Muttley from *The Wacky Races*?

JON: (ADOPTS DROLL NORTHERN DOGGY BROGUE) Er, no.

STEVE PUNT: What about Churchill, the dog from the Churchill Insurance advert?

JON: Ohhh, YES.

MOST INANE UTTERANCE ON LOCAL COMMERCIAL RADIO

'If you were a shoe, what type of shoe would you be and why?'
Spoken by mid-morning DJ Rik Lazer on The Buzzard FM.

MOST CRAPPY, CHEAP TV FORMAT PURCHASED IN QUICKEST TIME BY SATELLITE TV CHANNEL

It is almost impossible to come up with a programme idea bad enough not to make it onto TV. (This is known as Partridge Syndrome, after the famous 'Monkey Tennis' pitching scene, most of which now looks barely exaggerated.)

In 2009 some TV executives gathered in an office at digital TV channel E4's headquarters in West London to listen to a pitch for a new TV idea from the sort of people who make the sort of programmes that make you want to go back in time to a room above Frith Street in Soho and push John Logie Baird out of the window, along with his new invention, before either of them could do any damage. This is the sort of (but for legal reasons not the *actual*) TV company that would make actual programmes called things like *The Gay Team*, *Date My Mom* or *Lily Allen and Friends* and who, along with several other companies, have come to personify everything that's wrong with modern television.

On the day in question they entered the office at 10 a.m. to pitch a game show in which a group of naked women armed with crossbows enter a dark maze inside which there are hidden 12 angry dwarfs with knives. Two hundred and fifty cameras would film their every move and there was to be no way out. It was to be called *THE KNIFE DWARFS VS NAKED WOMEN MAZE*.

At 10.01 a.m. they had decided to commission 13 programmes for E4's summer schedules. The only question asked by the channel executives during the pitch was 'Who's hosting it?'. Once the magic words 'Vernon' and 'Kay' had been uttered, it was a shoe-in. The whole process had taken less than a minute, beating the record of 1 minute 6 seconds previously held by some utter shite called *Ghost Hunting with Girls Aloud* which genuinely aired on ITV 2 in 2006.

Other ideas that made it onto TV within moments of being pitched are:

★ Grannies Do The Filthiest Things

★ John Craven's Booze Round

★ Scooby Don't

★ Bill Oddie Watch

★ One Man and his Dogging

★ The Sky at Day

★ Corporate Fraud She Wrote

★ How Clean is Your Spouse?

★ Where Do You Think You Are?

★ The 5 to 10 O'Clock News

★ Ostenders

WORLD'S EASIEST JOB FOR AN INVESTIGATIVE JOURNALIST

Of course not all investigative journalists can be like John Pilger, Carl Bernstein or Bob Woodward, digging deep at great personal risk to expose the evils of society, taking on sinister corporate or governmental forces ranged against them and, in the case of Woodward and Bernstein, bringing down an American administration in the process. There simply aren't enough stories of that magnitude, but as I watched the *Panorama* investigation on the not-so-little story of the mess that is RBS I found myself thinking that JEREMY VINE must have the easiest job in journalism and possibly the whole of show-business. How it works is this: he turns up, always to the same place, an office block with a fountain outside which looks suspiciously like it might be the BBC building in White City, as though someone has said 'Could we not shoot you outside somewhere a bit different, Jeremy?' and he has gone, 'Well, you know I would, but I have to be back at Radio 2 in ten minutes, so I would rather not.' Then they say 'Well, it's not much of a *Panorama* if you are just sitting outside this same office block every week,' and he's gone 'Shut Up,' although it is hard to imagine him being that rude, and then he just says about three sentences to camera, looking really serious, and pisses off again while they show a film he has had no part in. He doesn't even have to do any actual investigating. He doesn't even take off his scarf, ever. You'd think for the credentials of the programme they might want someone a bit harder hitting anyway, like Wogan or Chris Evans. And then the whole programme was about how Fred Goodwin is getting something for doing nothing and I'm thinking . . . HD

MOST UNFORTUNATE INTERACTIVE SUGGESTION MADE BY BBC NEWS 24

'If you want to know more about the effects of North Korea's nuclear testing programme, press the RED BUTTON.'

MOST VOYEURISTIC PRETEND 'SOCIAL EXPERIMENT' TV PROGRAMME

PRIVATE MOMENTS A psychologist, a socio-economist and a New Age therapist watch through a hidden camera in the female changing-room of a typical British leisure centre. By analysing the way the women undress, their choice of underwear, and careful deconstruction of the close-fitting lycra outfits they choose to exercise in, they are able to paint a revealing picture of the pressures and body-image worries of modern British women. Made by Channel 4.

STONERS In order to understand more fully the effect of drugs and the lazy preconceptions we have about their use, a group of attractive young people are given a coffee-table full of skunk, papers, pure cocaine and E tablets, and told to enjoy themselves. Through a hidden camera, their responses are watched by a psychologist, a pharmacologist, and Justin Lee Collins (See *LOOKALIKES, WORLD'S BEST*). A serious examination of an important issue. Made by Channel 4.

TIME TEAM MINDF**K Unknown to Tony Robinson and
the team, Derren Brown has arranged subliminal signals
around their archaeological dig. On day 1 they begin to develop
a creeping sense of fear that they are being watched. On day 2
they begin to see visions of dead witches and headless monks.
On day 3 they are slowly driven insane as the inescapable evil of
the unhallowed graves in which they are digging begins to drive
them to madness and suicide. Through a hidden camera, Derren
watches and giggles. Made, obviously, by Channel 4.

THE SONNTAG NACHT PROJECT Were the Nazi
experiments really as bad as we make out? Here, some of the
less contentious experiments are reconstructed by a team of
historians in an attempt to help a modern audience understand
this dark period of the 20th century. In part 1, a young man is
placed in icy water for 20 minutes and then made to lie next to
two naked women in an attempt to see how fast he warms up.
The Nazis really did this to test the effects on pilots of ditching
in cold water. We're doing it as a valuable aid to historical
understanding. (Ratings for this show broke records for
Channel 4.)

MOST UBIQUITOUS YET VACUOUS TV PRESENTER

This is an extremely toughly fought category. Evidence suggests
that the record-holder could be any one of the dozens of
pointless lightweight entertainment puppets that are splattered
across our screens at any given time. Fortunately, scientists have

come up with a mathematical formula which has only recently enabled record-book adjudicators to work this out. The key is as follows:

t $\qquad$ = talent

a(x) $\qquad$ = number of television appearances (number in brackets)

> $\qquad$ = more famous than

< $\qquad$ = less famous than

$\neq$ $\qquad$ = does not equal

» $\qquad$ = ubiquitousness

+/- v $\qquad$ = plus or minus level of vacuity

$(\cdot)(\cdot)$ = Jordan

$[\cdot][\cdot]$ = Fearne Cotton

Using this formula the world record for most ubiquitous yet vacuous TV presenter can be worked out using the following equation:

t = -vvvvvvvv < $(\cdot)(\cdot)$ x a(∞) + UUUUU a(∞) = Tess Daly

(The mathematical symbol for Tess Daly = v)

Thus, most mathematicians now agree that Tess Daly is truly a vacuum inside a posh frock. Even more so than if you somehow squashed a Dyson All Floors into a fuchsia pink Martin Grant strapless dress and let it present a dancing show with Bruce Forsyth.

WORST PLACES FOR DOCTOR WHO'S POLICE BOX TO MATERIALISE

★ The G20 Anti-Capitalism Riots, London, 2 April 2009

★ The Battle of Orgreave, Orgreave Coking Plant Rotherham, UK Miners' Strike, 18 June 1984

★ Glastonbury Festival, any year – it could be mistaken for a loo

★ The Valley of Death, Balaclava, Crimea, 25 October 1854

★ Hiroshima, Japan, 8.14 a.m., 6 August 1945

★ The Fast Lane of the M6, any Friday night

★ Toxteth, Liverpool, 5 July 1981

EARLIEST SIGHTING OF A CHRISTMAS TV COMMERCIAL

Christmas now covers a full sixth of the year. As far as shops and advertisers are concerned, it starts the day after Bonfire Night and ends on Twelfth Night. That's 6 November to 6 January – two whole months. Television commercials are nothing but Santas and snow and sleigh bells from early November. This is not only unimaginative but also plain wrong – in Britain it generally snows in late January or early February. This has been the case *my whole life*, even when I was at school. I had a day off from school for snow in 1980, and that was in *February*. (Apologies to readers in Scotland, who probably do get snow before Christmas; but in the south, 2009's pre-Christmas snow came as such a shock *that the Channel Tunnel stopped working*. This didn't feature in any adverts.)

Last year, my local DIY shop was full of Christmas trees by *20 November*. What kind of lunatic buys a Christmas tree in mid-November? The sort who likes hoovering pine needles out of their carpet? Or the sort of chav idiot who thinks that making your terraced house into an Argos version of Blackpool's Golden Mile should be achieved at least two months before Christmas?

All the major supermarkets are wishing us 'Merry Christmas' a full two weeks before Advent. Since you, Reader, are a person who buys books, you probably know what Advent is, but many people think that the start of *I'm A Celebrity Get Me Out Of Here* is the biblical sign that the saviour is coming, and it is these people, presumably, who are the target of the retailers who have insisted that Christmas now lasts most of the autumn. But does anybody, in this day and age, seriously think they have to food-shop over a month in advance? Surely even the dimmest, fattest couch-potatoes in the land have worked out that shops are open right up to Christmas Eve and open again early Boxing Day, and that if you live in any size of town, there are plenty of shops open over Christmas anyway?

However, there are culprits who start advertising even earlier. For some years now, supermarkets have started putting Christmas products on the shelves in September, and it is not unknown to spot your first Santa or snow-scene on a TV commercial *before 1 October*. If this happens, make a note of the company that has made the commercial, and make a vow *never, ever to buy any of their products ever again*.

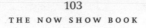

BIGGEST TV DETECTIVE CLICHÉ

All murder mysteries are essentially the same, and tend to rely on various plot devices which help tell them apart from real-life murders. The first giveaway is *murderers who get in touch*, preferably by phoning up the police station in a breathy voice and taunting the detective before getting off the line just quickly enough to avoid being traced. In real life this pretty much never happens, and when it does, it's usually a hoax anyway.

The next most-loved cliché is the nutter's den. In real life, very few murderers devote a whole room of their house to making a sort of shrine to their victims. They don't do this because frankly it would be a bit of a giveaway. On TV, however, most murderers have a handy nutter's den in the house, making it easy for the audience to know early on which of the suspects is the right one.

The biggest cliché, though, is THEMED MURDERS. Very few real-life criminals adopt a thematic approach, but TV ones invariably do. 'Wait a minute! The first victim's name was Matthew, right? And the second one was Mark?' 'My God! We'd better warn every Luke and John in the country!'

In real life, any serial-killer adopting an obvious thematic link between victims would be caught very quickly. In TV and film this doesn't happen, because the detectives are always completely ignorant of anything outside police work. They sit around in a police station staring at walls full of Post-it notes and photos going 'The first victim was Scott Smith. Then there was Virgil Brown. Then Alan Taylor. Then Gordon Trott . . .' and everybody shakes their heads. It then transpires that Scott was found floating in a swimming pool and Virgil was crushed by a collapsing palm tree, and *still* no one gets it. It's only when they remember that Alan was run over by a pink Rolls-Royce, and that Gordon was found suspended by strings from a wooden beam that light finally dawns.*

*Plot idea turned down by ITV as 'too realistic'.

WORST TV SITCOM PREMISE (UNTRANSMITTED PILOT)

The lamest premises for a situation comedy are those whose title incorporates the name of the character into a well-used phrase or saying to 'amusing' effect; *Nelson's Column* (BBC 1 sitcom starring John Gordon Sinclair as a newspaper columnist called Nelson), or more recently *The Life of Riley* starring Caroline Quentin as Maggie Riley whose life isn't going as easily as she'd like and this means that, despite being called Riley, she quite literally isn't living 'the life of riley'. It is from this 'amusing' juxtapostion that the so-called humour arises. With this in mind, the following contenders are legendary among the few who have seen them.

STICKS AND STONES WILL BREAK MY BONES

Eddie Sticks and Brian Stones are two friends who work in an abattoir and are in charge of the bone-crushing machine. With hilarious consequences.

THERE'S NO SMOKE WITHOUT FIRE

Eddie Smoke goes on holiday for the first time without his friend Brian Fire. But his friend Brian tracks him down and won't leave him alone.

THE SKY'S THE LIMIT

Eddie Sky and Brian Limit are two astronauts who live on the Isle of Skye where their Sky+ box has broken for the eighth time and now they've really run out of patience.

A STITCH IN TIME

Two seamstresses find a magical sewing machine that can transport them to the past. Their names are Maggie Stitch and Maggie Time.

FREE AS A BIRD

Eddie Bird is released from prison and joins a Paul Rodgers tribute band

SHEPHERD'S DELIGHT

Brian Shepherd is arrested for worrying sheep with a blancmange-like dessert

RHYTHM IS A DANCER

Maggie Rhythm is a dancer. With hilarious consequences.

MOST BAFFLING COMMERCIAL

A man in a gorilla suit sits waiting for the big drum intro on Phil Collins' 'In the Air Tonight'. The track is a three-chord classic; the drums (featuring the characteristic early-80s 'gated' effect, where the natural reverb of the drum is cut off sharply, producing a hollow sound) are highly distinctive. They don't come in until the closing fade of the track, giving the whole thing a suspenseful, slightly sinister feel; this matches the intended effect, of a couple's final, tumultuous row breaking out and ending the relationship.

What any of this has to do with a bar of chocolate, God alone knows. It's just a big show-off load of meaningless arse, based around a heartfelt song about a marriage breaking up. If you said 'Oh, what a great ad!' then you're an idiot.

MOST SPLENDID COMMERCIAL

The meerkat with the strange East European accent (whose website keeps getting confused with one that sells car insurance) held this position for a year or so, before they jumped the shark with it and went totally over the top. Even worse, it was directly responsible for Go Compare changing their commercials from a dull couple wandering about inside a laptop, to a loud comedy opera tenor sonically molesting people. These are, unquestionably, Britain's least popular ads. And yes, I am including the creepy little boy who wants to 'do a poo at Paul's house'. What Paul thinks about this hijacking of his lav, we simply don't know.

(See also *WORLD'S MOST APPARENTLY-STANDING-UP QUADRUPED*.)

MOST ORDERS FOR AWNINGS PLACED DURING AN ADVERTISING BREAK IN THE MIDDLE OF *COUNTDOWN*

Channel 4's weekday afternoon quite-dull-school-lesson-on-the-telly began life as the network's first programme in 1982. Then presented by real-life married couple Richard Whiteley and Carol Vorderman, the programme was on at a time when most of the people watching were either dead or dying, and as a result the adverts in the middle were (and quite possibly still are) for things like life insurance for the over-80s and, for some reason, awnings. The gaps in the middle of *Countdown* are in fact the main outlet for advertising that features awnings anywhere in the Western hemisphere, and so many are gathered here together that naturalists are able to use these advert breaks to check the migratory herding patterns of sun shade-based marketing.

However, despite them being seen in large numbers all year round, not one awning has ever been ordered as a result. Thus the record for Most Orders for Awnings Placed During an Advertising Break in the Middle of *Countdown* is NONE.

MOST DEVOTED FANS

Many bands, TV shows and movies have loyal fan bases, sometimes verging into mental illness. The officially recognised Most Devoted, though, are *STAR TREK* FANS. These are generally – and erroneously – broken down into two main sub-groups: Trekkies and Trekkers. While most people outside the sphere of *Star Trek* fandom regard the distinction as largely academic, there are in fact specific technical differences between the two denominations; moreover there exists a third subgroup whose existence is not widely known among the 'lay' population*.

The distinctions can, broadly speaking, be expressed as follows:

★ The kind of *Star Trek* fan who will watch *Star Trek* if it happens to be on TV, owns a few *Star Trek* DVDs and has been to one or two *Star Trek* conventions can be safely classed as a **Trekker**.

★ The kind of *Star Trek* fan who will never miss *Star Trek* on TV despite owning every series on DVD already, who attends every *Star Trek* convention they can possibly get to, always attends in full Starfleet costume and speaks fluent Klingon is known as a **Trekkie**.

★ Then we have the third level of *Star Trek* fans. These people believe that *Star Trek* is actually 100% literally true, and live their lives accordingly. These people are known as **Scientologists**.

---

*'Lay' here applies to non-*Star Trek* fans. It rarely applies to *Star Trek* fans in any sense.

MOST INCOMPETENT CARTOON VILLAIN

The worst cartoon baddie record has been held by DICK DASTARDLY since 1968. Every week on *The Wacky Races* he would take the lead in the race and be miles ahead of everyone else, but then he would waste hours stopping and rigging up an enormous anvil to drop off the edge of a cliff. This would entail a complex counterweight system which, given that his only physical assistance came from Muttley, must have taken a while to construct. Why he didn't just keep going, given that he had a rocket-powered car to start with, is not at all clear.

WORST BBC RADIO 4 SITCOM

INCURIEABLE!
The zany life of Marie Curie and her long-suffering husband as she tries to discover the secret of radioactivity while he does the dishes and looks after the kids!

'A clever and witty twist on the domestic comedy of role reversal, work-life balance and incurable disease' *Independent*

BEST COMPLAINT TO
THE NOW SHOW

In an early edition of the programme, Mr Hugh Dennis did a
joke about Colonel Gaddafi. The joke praised him for still being
a Colonel. 'You'd think, since he runs the country, by now he'd
have promoted himself.' It went on to contrast this with her
Majesty the Queen, 'Calls herself Commander-in-Chief of the
Armed Forces but hasn't even done basic training.'

An absolutely *furious* letter of complaint arrived from a
listener, pointing out that the Queen had done military service
during the war. This is, of course, true, and he had a point.
Although 'basic training' was six weeks of square bashing and
rifle drill, and we don't know if the Queen did that.

However, Princess Elizabeth certainly did serve as an auxiliary
ambulance driver during the war, so we conceded that the joke
was inaccurate. It was worth getting the complaint though,
because the complaint was funnier than the sketch. 'Not only
did Her Majesty serve during the war,' the letter read, 'but both
she and her sister Margaret can strip and reassemble an engine
in 20 minutes.'

WORST NIGHT OF VIEWING EVER ON THE SKY PLANNER

Those with Sky television will be familiar with its easy-to-use, at-a-glance, strip-along rundown of an evening's viewing. Laid out in a blue and yellow guide, the entertainment offerings of all channels with times and titles is available to see at the push of a button. It handily allows one to skim across a whole evening's viewing, which means that the cavalcade of unwatchable toss that passes for television these days is spread out in front of you like a carpet, though a sort of garish, unpleasant televisual carpet that someone's trodden the viewing equivalent of dog shit all over. Naturally our nation's TV schedules often throw up programmes in the form of unwatchable turds, but the evening of WEDNESDAY 13 MAY 2009 really did surpass itself. The roll call of dumbed-down rubbish that was on offer read like a kind of anti-*Schindler's List* of programmes that should under no circumstances be saved or led to safety. There was nothing on that could be considered even remotely watchable by any right-thinking human person.

The ordinarily reliable BBC2 had *Cash in the Celebrity Attic* (W – as I believe the 'kids' might say –TF???), BBC1 had something called *Fix My Fat Head* which I can only assume was a programme that was on loan from BBC3. BBC3 itself (from which one should never expect too much) had something like *Look At These Crap Tits* (or *Horne and Corden*, as they called it) and *Two Pints of Lager And A Packet Of Sodding Crisps* (a s[h]itcom which repeats on you more than actual lager) or some sort of inadequate sketch show which ticked none of the funny boxes but all of the ethnic-diversity ones. Channel 4 had yet another extreme freak show called, oh I dunno, *The Skin Whose Boy Fell Out* or something (presumably a sequel to the noted documentary *The Boy Whose Skin Fell Off* but this time from an alternative perspective). Channel 5 isn't even worth mentioning and ITV had, well, *The British Soap Awards*, a pointless cavalcade of such excruciating bland mediocrity that your eyes, rather than watch any more than 20 seconds of it, would voluntarily leave your head, crawl across the floor and attempt to drown themselves in your cup of hot tea. And that's even before Fearne Cotton turned up and started bleating down the camera.

In the face of stiff competition then, this was by far the worst night of viewing on the Sky Planner for quite some time. Although by the time you're reading this, there's probably been worse.

(See *CRAPPY, CHEAP TV FORMAT PURCHASED IN QUICKEST TIME BY SATELLITE TV CHANNEL*.)

THINGS THAT HAPPEN IN TOM AND JERRY

The records for things that happen in Tom and Jerry currently stand as follows:

- ★ Tom is tricked into whacking his own tail with a mallet (3,215 incidents)

- ★ Jerry minces out of his hole and does a double-take when he sees Tom's latest contraption (2,745)

- ★ Tom sees a lady cat and his eyeballs become heart-shaped and start throbbing (2,475)

- ★ Jerry dusts off his hands like the cunning, self-righteous little bastard he is (1,798)

- ★ Tom finishes eating a fish and leaves perfect complete fish-skeleton on plate (1,539)

- ★ Jerry found in trap with neck broken (0)

THE RECORD FOR PERSON MOST WILLING TO BE LIKE JEREMY CLARKSON

Is held by the meat-faced, enviro-thug himself. Clarkson has achieved this because even the most ignorant *Top Gear* mug is capable of envying Clarkson's simplistic, selfish, moronic take on the world and his car driving job without ever actually wishing to be him. MB

MOST COMPLAINTS ABOUT JONATHAN ROSS

To Prince Charles: 'So, was Princess Di a good shag, or did she have to keep running off to be sick?' (2,476 complaints)

To Nelson Mandela: 'So, did anything nasty ever happen in the prison showers?' (4,276 complaints)

To Ann Widdecombe: 'You say you're a virgin – but are you counting handjobs?' (5,286 complaints)

MOST EFFECTIVE WILD ANIMAL TO RELEASE INTO THE BIG BROTHER HOUSE

For a while opinions were divided as to what animal this would be, largely due to the ambiguity of the record title itself. For instance, the most effective animal at swinging on a tyre and throwing its own poo at the rest of the housemates would be a chimpanzee, or Bubble from series two. Similarly, the animal that would most fit in personality-wise is a toad, given that toads are largely nocturnal, are unpleasant to look at and would be better off held under the surface of a pond. But if we take into account most right-thinking people's opinion of *Big Brother* and its housemates and add that to what most of us would like to see happen to the people inside the *Big Brother* house live on camera, then the most effective wild animal to release into the *Big Brother* house would be an angry gorilla with a gun.

ARTS
AND
LITERATURE

WORST-RESEARCHED NOVEL

Dan Brown is not known for the quality of his research, but crucially, it's *only when he writes about something you have personal knowledge of* that you realise this. I'm not that big on early religion, medieval symbolism, Masonic history, particle physics, etc, so I will happily swallow all that. However, Chapter 44 of *Angels and Demons* takes place at the BBC, putting me in a position to question its factual accuracy with some authority. The following quibbles are noted –

1 The location of Broadcasting House is wrong.

2 The location of the newsroom is wrong. (It had moved from Broadcasting House to White City two years before the book was written.)

3 The terminology and job titles are wrong. (They're American, unsurprisingly.)

4 The person answering the phone is smoking, which was banned in all BBC buildings years before the book was written.

5 The BBC's Rome Correspondent is a new guy the BBC had picked up from some trashy tabloid. If there is an example of the BBC sending an inexperienced print journalist to cover a Papal Election, then I'm not aware of it. Unless Huw Edwards was picked up from a trashy tabloid. He doesn't look the type though.

6 The chapter ends with a BBC news editor *giving out the private number of the journalist to a total stranger*. It is essential to the plot of the book that this happens, but it never

would. The BBC do not give out private numbers, ever. You can't just phone them up and say, 'I've got a story about banks. Can I speak to Robert Peston please?' They won't put you through. They'll say something like, 'You'll have to speak to a researcher, Robert's at his weird voice class.'

All in all, the entire chapter is wrong with pretty much everything, which made me wonder about all the other chapters set in places I *haven't* worked in for twenty years. It is quite possible, of course, that Chapter 44 of *Angels and Demons* is an aberration, and that everything else Brown has written is scrupulously accurate. He was, of course, spot on about Jesus.

MOST CONTROVERSIAL CHILDREN'S BOOKS

You can find controversy in almost anything these days, and even the most innocuous children's literature is subject to criticism from pressure groups.

THE MR MEN
A nightmarish world of monomaniacal neurotics, each with one dominant trait that dictates their entire personality. Instead of sending them all to The Priory for counselling, they are left to roam around making each other's lives a misery. The books are regularly updated, however, and it's possible that, at some point, Mr Bump will make a fortune from Accident Compensation Direct; Mr Grumpy will be prescribed medication; and Mr Tickle will be put on the Sex Offenders' Register.

THE VERY HUNGRY CATERPILLAR

A hymn to obesity and poor diet. The hero of the book begins by eating a healthy fruit-based diet and within a week is consuming cherry pie, cupcakes and sausages. As a result of this, 'he had a stomach ache'. This sends out a message to children that the only downside of such an appalling diet is a bad tummy. Health campaigners have suggested that the caterpillar should turn into a butterfly that is unable to take off. In an attempt to get his massive bulk off the ground, he flaps his wings so violently that he has a heart attack.

Over-eating, though, is probably better than not eating at all, and plans had to be shelved for the follow-up, *The Slightly Anorexic Centipede*.

THOMAS THE TANK ENGINE

Locomotive-based morality tales, hypnotically attractive to very small boys. The general message of Thomas is that conformity makes you happy. Being cheeky, proud, diesel-engined, or different in any way (i.e. a bus) will lead to misery. There is one story in which a naughty engine is bricked-up into a tunnel, an image so traumatic that even dads find themselves waking up screaming.

ANGELINA BALLERINA

People always complain that girls have make-up, boys and general rubbish shoved down their throats far too young, but the reason this happens is that they are desperate to escape the pink-themed world of Disneyfied girly tat that they are force-fed when younger. It's not surprising that girls go surly and emo when they hit their teens; they have spent their first decade in a massive trough of emetic feminine stereotyping that defies belief. Everything for little girls is a) pink and b) involves cutesy animals and ballet. Hence the huge success of Angelina Ballerina, who is a ballet-dancing mouse. I'll say no more.

MOST CONTROVERSIAL CHRISTMAS BOOK

Undoubtedly, the most controversial Christmas book ever published is RICHARD DAWKINS' *THE SANTA DELUSION*, in which he argues that Father Christmas does not exist. The sudden appearance overnight of perfectly matched presents for every child in the world had long puzzled humanity, and for many years this apparently miraculous phenomenon was ascribed to Santa Claus flying around the globe on a sleigh pulled by reindeer, distributing the presents from a big sack.

Scientists, sceptical of the practicalities of this in the short timescale involved, devised a different theory. They called the process 'parental selection', and caused outrage among believers everywhere. 'Parental selection' is a slow and gradual process, taking many months, in which the child's likes and dislikes are noted and a range of presents gradually assembled and purchased from various sources.

This idea was fiercely opposed by believers in Santa, of which there are two types. Fundamentalists believe in what is called 'Toy Creationism' – the belief that Santa creates all the toys himself, in a secret factory at the North Pole, assisted by a workforce of elves. This theory stood for many years until it was gradually undermined by the growth of branded and packaged goods. By the 1960s it was increasingly difficult to argue that Action Man had been made in Santa's own factory, when it could be clearly observed that he was trademarked and marked 'Made in England. Die-hards stuck to the theory, but many children grew cynical about the existence of Father Christmas, refusing to believe that elves could construct replica Hornby sets or Sindy dolls, let alone shrink-wrap them in plastic.

Faced with this, Santa believers devised a new version of their belief, known as 'Intelligent Delivery'. This accepted the notion that the toys themselves may have been created by different companies in different countries around the world, but argued that their distribution on Christmas Eve was still accomplished overnight by a single individual on a flying sleigh.

Scientists fought back against the idea of an Intelligent Deliverer, pointing out that many of the assumptions made by believers were flawed. Many houses, for example, lack chimneys and fireplaces, giving nowhere for Santa to gain entry. The speed required to visit every child in one night would exceed all known laws of physics, and experiments have proved that reindeer do not, under any known circumstances, possess the power of flight, and lack any means of generating sufficient aerodynamic lift to do so. The appearance of presents on Christmas morning, say scientists, can only be explained by parental selection – although this does not mean that the Santa story is not wonderful, and many scientists have told it to their own children.

None of this has deterred believers in the Intelligent Deliverer, who claim that the scientists lack evidence for their theory. 'If, as scientists believe, these presents are being put there by parents, then why have so few children ever witnessed this?' they ask – and this is a tricky question to answer. Many children also leave out a glass of sherry for Santa and a carrot for Rudolf, and these are visibly gone in the morning. 'Do these so-called scientists seriously suggest that grown adults would surreptitiously remove a carrot in the middle of the night merely to maintain a deceptive charade?' they argue. 'The scientific version removes all the beauty and meaning of Christmas.'

This controversy has raged for many years, especially in America, but has become more prominent recently due to plans to teach Intelligent Delivery in schools, as an 'alternative theory'. This, say proponents, is to prevent the children of Toy Creationist households from being 'offended' when taught that Santa does not exist. Astonishingly, nearly a quarter of science teachers say that they harbour a residual belief in Santa themselves, 'because it's such a lovely idea'. They refuse, however, to teach children that the world was created in six days by a man with a beard, because 'that's just mental'.

WORLD'S FUNNIEST BOOK

(Apart from this one, obviously.) The World's Funniest Book is – cleerly – reckognized by all DISCERNING TYPES hem hem and will need NO INTRODUKTION what is that you sa molesworth 2? You are betraying yore middle-class upbringing and the fakt that you hav read your mater and pater's copy as a child? I do not kare. The funniest book is obviously molesworth and all agree even fotherington-thomas, who hav read the TWILIGHT TRILOGY boo hiss becos he is utterly wet and weed and like books for GURLS hem hem. The best thing about molesworth of course is that it is not a SHAMELESS SPIN-OFF from some radio or tv show. Coo er gosh are you being post-modern and self-refferential Molesworth sa peason. No you clot, I riposte, just angling for a mention in the broadsheets go on o you mite. Not a chance he sa, not with new zadie smith and more war memoirs due out. Not to mention my divorce by Jordan.

LONGEST JOKE

All jokes told on the BBC are now much longer than they used to be, owing to the internal requirements of the Corporation. The current world's longest joke is:

Q: How many BBC employees does it take to change a lightbulb?

A: We are all about change! However, the bulb can only be changed once assessed for Health and Safety, and provided the new lightbulb is sourced from a Preferred Supplier to the relevant Department, and that requisitioning and payment for the new lightbulb has been submitted and approved via the appropriate channels to both your departmental manager, line manager and financial controller. Once this has been signed off by at least two senior departmental executives, and providing the new lightbulb is fully compliant (compliance to be obtained and ratified prior to any invoicing thereof), and providing that the new lightbulb is requisitioned via the SAP system and conforms to all current policies on ethnic, sex and age discrimination, the lightbulb can then be changed by approved personnel from a Preferred Maintenance Outsource Supplier, provided this is budgeted for under the guidelines currently in force regarding lightbulbs and the changing thereof within the current financial year.

Sadly, it's only really funny if you don't have to work there.

WORLD'S
OLDEST JOKE

Archaeologists have discovered a Stone-Age cave-painting in
the Vezere Valley, France, which appears to show two human
figures and a dog without a nose. This is believed to be around
30,000 years old. In 1926, Egyptologist Howard Harker reported
discovering hieroglyphics inside the Pyramid of Cheops which
also appeared to read 'My dog has no nose', but attributed this
to the process of mummification, during which the brains would
be scooped out through the nasal cavity. Sadly, the remaining
lines of the inscription were eroded away, so we will never know
if the remainder read, 'How does he smell? Terrible.' Or, 'It was
removed so that he may join the Pharaoh in the afterlife.'

The oldest definitely recorded version of the 'chicken crossing
the road' joke comes from Thomas Middleton's 1602 play, *Thrice
Fie Upon Thee*, where the apothecary Patcher says to Sir James
Limwort:

PATCHER: Wherefore, sirrah, did yon chicken traverse the
highway?

LIMWORT: I'faith, I know not.

PATCHER: Why, sir, for he desireth nought else but to reach
th'opposing pavement.

LIMWORT: 'Tis a pretty riddle, aye, and a merry one.

PATCHER: I did hear Barry Cryer tell it 'pon Michaelmas last.

MOST MISQUOTED PHRASE

'*Suffer little children*' is invariably used when children are suffering. As a headline, it always means a horrible story about abuse/murder/bullying. However, the word 'suffer' here means 'to allow or permit', a common usage at the time this sentence was written – in the 17th century, for the King James Bible. 'Suffer the little children to come unto me,' just means, 'Hey, let the kids get up close and personal,' only Jesus didn't talk like that. (Unless you have a really trendy vicar.) However, the world's most-misquoted phrase is:

'*THE WORLD IS MY OYSTER*'. Invariably used to mean 'the world is at my feet' or 'I can go wherever I want', which is not what it means at all. In Shakespeare's *The Merry Wives of Windsor*, Sir John Falstaff says to the vainglorious idiot Pistol, 'I shall not lend thee a penny,' to which Pistol replies, 'Why then, the world's mine oyster, which I with sword will open.' An oyster is not something luxurious, it is something that has to *be prised open with a blade*. The phrase means, 'I will have to use force to get what I want.'

Basically it's a line about knife-crime and how it gets results. It is, therefore, slightly odd that Transport for London chose to call its travel-pass the Oystercard. They were clearly under the impression that it means 'you can go wherever you want', whereas, in fact, taken literally, an Oystercard entitles you to stab anyone you want on public transport. It's quite impressive the number of London teenagers who take it this way; clearly Shakespeare is more popular with hoodies than is commonly thought.

WORLD'S MOST CRIMINALLY OVERRATED MOVIE

Many people are disappointed by *CITIZEN KANE*, Orson Welles's 1941 movie debut, which for over half a century regularly topped critics' lists. It's a MacGuffin-based thriller around the idea that we can never truly know what drives some people to greatness, especially if the answer is 'a sledge'.

There are, however, many runners-up in this field. Other people have an intense dislike of *Titanic*, the world's most popular film and Oscar-winner. However, it does display James Cameron's talent for the truly mythic story. Obviously it's no *Terminator 2*, but then what is? (Certainly not *Terminator 3*, which was arse.)

Also regularly nominated for the Most Over-Rated category is the second *Star Wars Trilogy*. George Lucas had made so much money from his original droid-a-thon he became convinced that rather than making a sci-fi romp, he was in fact making a profound mythical exploration of the nature of evil. This is never a good thing (see *ALL HARRY POTTER BOOKS APART FROM THE FIRST ONE*).

The point of the prequels was to 'explain Darth Vader's journey to the dark side' – in other words, a profound mythical exploration of the nature of evil. This is the same task that defeated Milton in *Paradise Lost* and, to be honest, it was never likely that George Lucas was going to succeed where the second-greatest 17th-century poet failed. Milton had a similar-sized ego – he proclaimed that he was writing 'things unattempted yet in prose or rhyme' and that his aim was 'to justify the ways of

God to men' – but at least he didn't come up with Jar Jar Binks. He also didn't write long stretches of interminable dialogue about intergalactic trade tariffs and the voting structure of the Federation. Lucas's exploration of the nature of evil came down to Anakin Skywalker dreaming that his wife was going to die in childbirth, and getting so cross about it that he killed everybody – a plot which, even 30 centuries ago in Ancient Greece at the very birth of drama would have had people saying, 'Euripides, mate, that's not really very convincing.'

MOST OVERUSED MOVIE PLOTS

3   A hopeless sports team/sportsman who have no money but are lovable and decent, have to take on a ruthless team of rich, soul-less jocks. This will enable them to win some money to give to an orphanage or pay for an operation or something lovable and decent. They are in despair when an ageing but well-remembered actor arrives to take over their training, and he turns them around. They go on to win. Will Ferrell is in it. The script is written by Microsoft American Comedy for Windows. (See MEDIA MYTH, BIGGEST.)

2   Someone gets a chance to meet themselves in the future / meet themselves in the past / turn into their own parent / swap places with their dog / go back in time and help their granddad meet their granny / go back one year and meet the writer of the movie and say, 'Did they really pay you to write this?'

1 A man kills his wife and then loses his memory – or does he? Maybe he's only pretending to lose his memory, so a top police psychologist is assigned to befriend him undercover – but then they, too, lose their memory! Hilarity ensues as the two amnesiac opposites try to remember which is the cop and which is the killer!

LONGEST-RUNNING PLAY

THE MOUSETRAP is the world's longest running play, and yet no one ever meets anyone who's ever seen it. It may not actually exist.

GREATEST SUPERHEROES

See *HOLLYWOOD GENRE, MOST OVERRATED*. All superheroes are basically the same, with minor variations. It's a comic-book genre, so-called because the characterisation is on a level with *The Beano*.

BATMAN Witnesses the killing of his parents. Blames himself. Devotes his life to alter-ego crime-fighting, using nocturnal flying mammal as model. Given the vast financial resources he pours into constructing a Batcave, customised car, helicopter and searchlight, you do wonder whether he couldn't have just made a big donation to the Gotham City Police Department, enabling them to employ some more police. Love interest works as a newspaper photographer.

SPIDER-MAN Witnesses the killing of his uncle. Blames himself. Devotes his life to alter-ego crime-fighting, using eight-legged arachnid as model. Lacking financial resources, he relies on special abilities conferred by bite from radioactive spider. Works as a newspaper photographer.

DAREDEVIL Witnesses the killing of his father. Devotes his life to alter-ego crime-fighting, relying on special abilities conferred by radioactive gunk that falls off the back of a lorry. Not a journalist, but does know one.

FANTASTIC FOUR In a radical move, the Fantastic Four don't have any dead relatives to avenge. They do, however, make the mistake of tangling with the sinister forces of radioactivity. In the superhero-comic world, this always causes bizarre but useful mutations – rather than, say, cancer. Exposure to cosmic radiation causes weird things to happen to them, (see *Godzilla, Quatermass, Incredible Shrinking Man, et al*) and they decide to devote their lives to alter-ego crime-fighting. What makes the Fantastic Four especially rubbish is that none of their superpowers are really very useful. Mr Fantastic is all stretchy, The Human Torch catches fire a lot, The Thing is just a thing, and Invisible Woman can become, er, invisible. They cast Jessica Alba to play her in the movies, meaning that they wanted her as visible as possible.

SUPERMAN Not actually human, thus not needing any radioactive exposure to develop superpowers. To make up for this, he works as a journalist, as does his girlfriend. The spread of mobile phones has been a big problem for him, as he now finds it increasingly difficult to find anywhere to get changed.

WORST
POET

It was, of course, Douglas Adams in *The Hitchhiker's Guide to The Galaxy* who famously pointed out that the worst poet in the universe, after all Vogons, was Paula Nancy Millstone Jennings of Greenbridge, Essex. But that's because Mr Adams inconveniently died before he'd had the misfortune to hear of MURRAY LACHLAN YOUNG. There are many, many things wrong with the poems of Murray Lachlan Young. For a start, they're written by someone called Murray Lachlan Young who sounds less like a poet and more like a cheap firm of solicitors. Although that would explain why the poems themselves sound like they were written by a cheap firm of solicitors. In the pub. After they've lost a case. And their minds.

We didn't get permission to reprint, here in *The Now Show Book*, a genuine Murray Lachlan Young poem about hair. Which isn't surprising, given that we were only going to slag it off. Why not google it instead and then read it out loud to yourself. Done it? Good. Now try telling me he's not a twat.

MOST QUOTED LINE FROM *GLADIATOR*

It's a choice of two, really. The most quoted line is probably 'On my command – unleash hell'. But the most quoted section is a whole speech – 'My name is Maximus Decimus Meridius, Commander of the Armies of the North, General of the Felix Legions, loyal servant to the true Emperor, Marcus Aurelius. Father to a murdered son, husband to a murdered wife. And I will have my vengeance, in this life or the next.'

However, these two lines are only the most quoted because, sadly, they cut the scene in which Maximus says, 'Oooh, these helmets are really butch!'

WORLD'S GITTIEST WIZARD

The world of wizardry is not left wanting for unlikeable, annoying and, frankly, gitty wizards. From Paul *Never Mind 'You'll Like This Not A Lot' Actually I Don't Even Like It One Tiny Bit* Daniels to the speccy, owl-worrying boy conjuror Harry Potter, the sawing-a-hat-in-half, pulling-a-dove-out-of-a-rabbit brigade have had it far too good for far too long. This has accidentally led to the position that society finds itself in now, which is one of watching magicians and tolerating them rather than burning them at the stake or drowning them using specially built stools.

Early attempts to become the world's gittiest wizard were attempted by the magician David Copperfield who claimed to have made New York's Statue of Liberty disappear on live television, when in fact he had done nothing of the sort but merely duped the audience with mirrors. He fell out of favour sometime in late 2001 after Osama bin Laden did it properly with the Twin Towers to a) a bigger TV audience and b) without any camera tricks.

The record, however, for the World's Gittiest Wizard is held by DAVID BLAINE, who also holds the record of the fastest man to drive Marcus Brigstocke to near apoplexy. Blaine's efforts at gitwizardry are many and include growing a twat's beard, being frozen in ice, hanging in a glass box and standing on a pole (instead of being tied to the end of it and held under water in the Middle Ages like his kind should be). It is for these reasons alone that the rest of *The Now Show* team do not allow Marcus anywhere near firearms.

THE RECORD FOR MOST MUNDANE AND POINTLESS LYRICS . . .

Is held by Lily Allen. This among some stiff competition is no mean feat, but Lily's determination to sing only about her own drab, tiresome, narrow vortex of an existence has seen her beat her competitors into a cocked hat. Ironically, she once wrote a whole album about a hat she once owned (records don't show if it had been cocked or not – quite possibly it had, knowing Lily). She thought she'd lost the hat, then found it again. It was very very funny indeed – this fact was confirmed by all her mates when she texted them to say it was in the cupboard all the time. MB

BIGGEST DISAGREEMENT AMONG *NOW SHOW* TEAM

Steve does not concur with Marcus (and Jon) about Lily Allen.
He regards 'The Fear' as one of the most intelligent lyrics to reach
No. 1 for a long time; a critique of celeb-driven consumerism
which simultaneously acknowledges its insidious attraction.
The plan is to sort this out once and for all – on Wandsworth
Common, using a choice of pistols or rapiers. Hugh will officiate,
and call the ambulance afterwards.

MOST IMPERSONATED, ERM, PERSON

The most impersonated person in the world is of course ELVIS
PRESLEY (1935–1977). There are currently over 400,000
professional Elvis impersonators in the world. Interestingly, at
the time of his death in 1977 there were only 170. This rate of
expansion of Elvis impersonation is such that were it to continue
at a constant rate, by the year 2020 it is estimated that *one third
of the world's population would be Elvis impersonators.*

It's interesting to note that had Elvis continued to expand at
the rate at which he himself was expanding at the time of his
death, then by the year 2020 one third of the world's population
by weight would be Elvis.

If we can assume – as do some 40 per cent of Americans –
that Elvis Presley is in fact alive if not especially well somewhere,
then we can extrapolate The Elvis Event Horizon, whereby:

One third of the human race is Elvis,
One third of the human race *thinks* it's Elvis,
And the remaining third is very bored and very hungry.

MOST INAPPROPRIATE THING SUGGESTED TO GO ON THE FOURTH PLINTH IN TRAFALGAR SQUARE

At the north-west corner of Trafalgar Square in London, UK, there is an empty plinth. The others are traditionally occupied by Generals or Kings or, in latter years, their statues. For instance, in 1808 King George, who by that time had gone mental, stood on the plinth nearest to what is now a Tesco Metro wearing a piece of turf on his head for four days while waving a carrot at the sky. He was taken down and replaced by a statue of Sir Charles James Napier, former Commander-in-Chief of the British Army in India.

The fourth plinth, however, has remained empty, but suggestions as to what it should hold have not been backward in coming forward. Of these, the most inappropriate things to go on the fourth plinth are:

- Another plinth. A fifth plinth.

- A statue of Carol Thatcher blacked up and holding a golliwog.

- A Starbucks.

- Public hangings.

- A wind turbine.

- The actor Tom Cruise explaining the benefits of scientology while bouncing up and down on a sofa.

- Sauron's Eye from *The Lord of the Rings*.

- A statue of Bono shedding a tear on behalf of the world's poor.

All of these ideas were considered by the Greater London Authority and dismissed on health and safety and/or religious grounds. They were superseded anyway by an idea posited in early 2009. Thus the record for the Most Inappropriate Thing Suggested To Go On The Fourth Plinth in Trafalgar Square is held by the weirdy artist Antony Gormley who announced plans to get members of the Great British Public to stand on it. Members of the Great British Public are notoriously fickle when it comes to visual demonstrations of pretentious, arty tosspottery (see WIZARD, WORLD'S GITTIEST) and thus the idea was considered to be a recipe for disaster. This happened quite literally later that year when meat-faced, food abuser Heston Blumenthal announced plans to cook the plinth and turn it into a poisonous soufflé. He fed the results to anyone who'd been standing on it and 28 days later 98 per cent of the world's population was dead.

GREATEST SINGLE

Bafflingly, despite the general loathing and contempt for prog rock, BOHEMIAN RHAPSODY often wins polls for the best single of all time. Everything about it is prog from its title onwards – the quasi-classical piano, the quasi-operatic singing, the bolted-together musical sections, the length, and the fact that it ends with a gong. It is in every way the kind of song that everyone normally hates. So why is it so popular? Answers on a postcard please.

MOST DIVA-ESQUE DEMANDS BY A FEMALE POP STAR

When pop stars are in town they often issue hotels and/or concert venues with a set of demands which can range from a specific brand of bottled mineral water (Madonna) all the way up to a kabbalah bracelet that's been dipped in some wind harvested from the top of Mount Everest that morning (Madonna). The current record, however, is currently held by Mariah Carey who, on her last visit to London, UK, demanded (and got) from her hotel the following list of items:

- A red carpet from the limousine to lead right through the hotel up to Ms Carey's suite and into the bed. (Bed must be made from the soft pelts of baby owls.)

- Celine Dion's head on a platter.

- A beautiful and rare white rhino to be held in captivity in Ms Carey's room until such time that Ms Carey deems it be released.

- A tribe of warrior monks.

- A horse.

- A horse whisperer.

- Two rounds of tuna and cucumber sandwiches.

- Twelve drummers drumming.

- A unicorn.

- Twelve unicorns drumming.

MOST SUCCESSFUL BAND OF ALL TIME

This is, obviously, THE BEATLES. Fans of overweight cabaret artist Elvis Presley still get cross about this, but they were.

Over 28 million books have been written about The Beatles, but new facts still emerge all the time:

- The Beatles had eleven drummers before they became famous, each drummer having bested the previous incumbent in physical combat. Ringo finally acceded to the drum stool after defeating Pete Best in a ten-round tickle fight.

- George Martin is perfectly capable of talking about subjects other than The Beatles, he simply chooses not to.

- If you play the outro to 'Strawberry Fields Forever' backwards, you can hear your stylus being ruined.

- Only two people have heard Revolutions 2 through 8, and they were both rendered hopelessly insane.

- Every year, 24,976 extremely stupid tourists are killed while being photographed on That Zebra Crossing.

- After 'splitting up', The Beatles continued to record throughout the 1970s under the names Badfinger, then Chas & Dave, Bob Marley and the Wailers and finally Dana.

- To this day, Ringo has no idea that The Beatles have split up. Every morning he arrives at Abbey Road studios and waits patiently at his drums until closing time, when he gives up and goes home, muttering 'Same time tomorrer then' to the receptionist.

BEST RIFF

By common consent the most famous riff of all time is that of 'SMOKE ON THE WATER', a track by Deep Purple from their 1971 album *Machine Head*. The lyric is based on a real-life incident of a hotel fire in the town of Montreux, where the band were recording, but stuff that, this isn't Wikipedia.

Quite why 'Smoke on the Water' became so famous is not clear. It's not the best track on *Machine Head* (that's 'Highway Star', obviously) and the most likely theory is the most obvious – it's *really bloody easy*.

The reason dud – dud – DAA, dud – dud, DA-DAAA is so famous is that it's very simple to play. Stick a bit of distortion on it and you don't even need to get all six strings. In fact, come to think of it, it's basically punk rock, five years too early.

Then have a go at 'Layla' and bring yourself back down to earth.

SILLIEST POP STAR'S CHILD'S NAME

There are many stupid pop stars, all of whom think it clever for some reason to bestow stupid names upon their unfortunate offspring. Famously these can range from the likes of Fifi Trixibelle Twinkletits Peshwari Naan Geldof all the way up to Peaches Starfruit Bananaman HB Pencil Kalashnikov Knitwear Geldof. It is not a new phenomenon. Over the years Frank Zappa has called his children Moon Unit and Dweezil and Hammer Time, while in 2004 Chris Martin out of Coldplay and his wife, the actress Gwyneth Paltrow out of films, had a Fairtrade baby and called it Oxfam. In 2006 the children's television programme *Blue Peter* held a competition for its audience to name the show baby, but it was later found the votes were rigged. During the night, someone had left the baby on Welsh presenter Gethin Jones and, just weeks after it became the show's pet, viewers voted for it to be called Spongebob. Sadly, producers decided to overrule this and instead the baby was named Socks The Cat. Everyone connected with this scandal was summarily executed on orders of BBC Oberführer Mark Thompson later that year.

The current silliest pop star child's name is the one bestowed on a Malawian orphan by MADONNA and then husband GUY RITCHIE in 2006. It's unpronounceable in any language but sounds a bit like 'Mwah' or something, which is less of a name and more the noise of a pretentious air kiss.

LEAST CHILD-FRIENDLY NURSERY RHYMES

Many of the nursery rhymes taught to the under-5s are horrible, and would never even get published if submitted as a children's book.

JACK AND JILL Two unsupervised children are sent off alone up a hill to fetch a pail of water. Both of them sustain injuries, Jack's being a skull fracture. With no apparent parent or responsible adult to care about him, he is forced to self-medicate, and goes to bed 'to mend his head with vinegar and brown paper'. This appalling tale of child neglect and injury is entirely unsuited to its intended audience.

THREE BLIND MICE A trio of disabled rodents are attacked and mutilated by a farmer's wife. Recommended rating 18.

DING DONG BELL A defenceless cat is thrown down a well by little Johnny Green. She is then rescued by Little Tommy Stout. The delinquent Green's only punishment is to be told that, 'What a naughty boy was that, to try and drown poor pussycat.' Frankly, a repeat offence is likely.

WHO KILLED COCK ROBIN? A police procedural for infants. An inquest is held on a dead bird. An eyewitness is sought, and a fly turns out to have seen the whole thing. As a suspense thriller, though, it's deeply flawed, as the culprit owns up straight away. A sparrow volunteers immediately that he killed cock robin and, what's more, he freely identifies the murder weapon (a bow and arrow). Not only violent, but poor story structure.

TOM, TOM, THE PIPER'S SON A truly bleak tale of theft, death and corporal punishment. Tom's father is clearly too busy piping to bother with parenting skills, given that his son is a hit-and-run pig-stealer. Quite why Tom stole the pig is unclear, but it's quite hard to run carrying a pig, and he is easily caught. The pig's relief, though, is temporary, as he is swiftly killed and eaten, while Tom is thrashed and 'went roaring down the street'. (Some modern versions say 'crying' which is even worse.) Would you buy your children a book called 'Smack the Pig-Thief'?

All in all, I'd say the PlayStation is just as useful for improving young minds.

WORST RHYMING COUPLET IN POP

Some people shouldn't be allowed to write songs. We'll take it as read that Pete Doherty should be locked in a box without a pencil and that Girls Aloud should have their hands tied and tongues glued to their lips so they can't even hum, but there are some stand-out couplets in modern pop music that really do make you wince whenever you hear them. And when I say 'wince' I actually mean 'actively want to track down the writer and beat them to death with a rhyming dictionary'.

It's by no means a new phenomenon. When Supertramp wrote 'Come on you little fighter / no need to get uptighter' in 'It's Raining Again' in 1982, they probably high-fived and went to the pub. What they should have done is popped along to a BTEC

Songwriting course at the local technical college. Not long after this, Duran Duran entered the cringey-face fray with 'The Reflex' and its dreadful couplet of 'And fiery demons all dance when you walk through that door / Don't say you're easy on me you're about as easy as a nuclear war', although that bit of hatefully robust hyperbole would doubtless survive a nuclear war along with cockroaches and Lily Allen. (Speaking of which see THE RECORD FOR MOST MUNDANE AND POINTLESS LYRICS SECTION.)

Lily's lyrics are clumsier than the Chuckle Brothers travelling to a Frank Spencer convention on roller skates towing Laurel and Hardy behind them on a grand piano. Still. It almost pales into insignificance compared to this:

> 'I don't want to see a ghost / It's the sight that I fear most /
> I'd rather have a piece of toast'

That's real. That's from Des'ree's 1988 hit 'Life'. It's a good job I'm not armed.

Now, while these examples are all very, very hateful, they do not hold the record for Worst Rhyming Couplet in Pop. No, for sheer breathtaking tastelessness and maximum 'Did I just hear that correctly?' factor the record is held by the 90s band Snap! and their dance-floor emptier 'Rhythm is a Dancer'. Ready? Here it comes:

> I'm as serious as cancer When I say rhythm is a dancer

Told you.

MUSICAL INSTRUMENT YOU LEAST WANT YOUR CHILD TO LEARN

Most parents are keen that their offspring should learn to play a musical instrument even if their child shows no musical prowess. However, three things should be borne in mind:

1   Unlike other extra-curricular activities such as sport, the learning of an instrument takes place mainly within the family home under the supervision of the parent.

2   The amount of practice specified by music teachers even for the lowliest grade exam makes the training programme of a teenage Chinese Olympic gymnast look pointlessly light.

3   Until the child has been playing for some years, the noise they make blowing, plucking, bowing or banging is akin to torture and was indeed used as such in Guantanamo Bay. When waterboarding proved ineffective, a seven-year-old would be brought into the cell and told to play the violin until a full confession had been extracted from the suspect. (This practice was, however, stopped when a guard who had forgotten to put on his ear defenders confessed full responsibility for 9/11, claimed he knew the whereabouts of Osama bin Laden and that he was himself the Commander-in-Chief of Al Qaida in the North-West Frontier. Since this time it has been illegal under the terms of the Geneva Convention for children to play 'Greensleeves' more than twice in interrogation situations.)

The lot of the parent can, however, be made much worse by allowing the child to choose an instrument that not only makes an appalling noise when played badly, but which is also *too large for the child to carry*, meaning that the child has to be transported everywhere. Therefore, the instruments you least want your child to learn are as follows:

THE CELLO Played badly it sounds like someone torturing a donkey. Light enough to carry, but big enough to kill a pensioner if carried by a child in a crowded street.

THE TUBA Impossible to play, impossible to listen to, and larger than the average child.

THE HARP The harp makes a lovely noise, but is impossible to transport anywhere without the aid of a fork-lift. You may also think that a Citroen Xsara, or Renault Espace will be big enough – it won't be. Parents who allow their children to learn the harp will find themselves swapping the little family run-around for a 16-wheeler at the very minimum. Parents should note that very little music has ever been written for the harp. Mozart thought about it apparently, but then decided that the bloody thing was simply too cumbersome to carry and he would leave it to a composer born after the invention of the internal combustion engine. On the one hand, this means that concerts for your child will be rare, but on the other, when they do happen they will be an awfully long way away – sometimes up to 1,000 miles – all of which you will have to drive very early on a Sunday morning in your juggernaut.

(See *SPORT YOU LEAST WANT YOUR CHILD TO BE GOOD AT.*)

MOST RIDICULOUS JAMES BOND MOVIE

Most people think Sean Connery was the best Bond – and most people, as usual, are wrong. The tax-dodging Scots curmudgeon was certainly a decent Bond – but there was no one to compare him with except the Bond in the books, and the Bond in the books is an emotionally retarded misogynist cretin. Seriously, any human being was going to look good as Bond compared with the book version. (Sample line from *The Spy Who Loved Me* – 'All women love semi-rape. They love to be taken.')

Given that the books are horrible, and that the hero is a creepy male-fantasy nightmare, the movies were bound to produce a nicer Bond. However, whether Sean Connery was the best of these is highly debatable. After the masterpiece of *Goldfinger* it was all downhill for him.

You Only Live Twice is only good for the last half-hour, once you see the volcano-based villain's lair; the rest of the film is rubbish, especially the long section where Connery is made to look Japanese in order to marry a Japanese woman. He doesn't look Japanese in the slightest; he looks like an ex-milkman from Edinburgh with a silly haircut. *Diamonds are Forever* is a ridiculous film, involving close-ups of cassettes, a gratuitous moon-buggy sequence (the Apollo missions were big in 1971) and a frankly homophobic pair of villains, Wint and Kydd – the Julian and Sandy of evil. The movie was saved by its iconic title song, the sublime instrumental called 'Capsule in Space'.

All of which brings us to the criminally underrated Roger Moore, always sneered at but frankly *Live and Let Die* knocks all but one of Connery's into a cocked hat. Not only does it have the best Bond theme ever, but it also has a non-stop roller-coaster of a plot, based around Yaphet Kotto (see *MOST UNDERRATED BOND VILLAIN WHO WAS IN MIDNIGHT RUN WITH ROBERT DE NIRO*). Yaphet Kotto is trying to flood America with cheap heroin in order to get the whole population addicted before jacking the prices up. How's that for the sordid reality of Nixon-era America? None of your stupid satellite-swallowing spaceships and megalomaniac world-dominators here. By Bond standards, it's a gritty, funny, all-action and strangely PC romp (the charismatic villains are black; the comedy relief is a redneck white sheriff).

Then the slide began. Moore's next Bond was *The Man with the Golden Gun*, which has the officially recognised Worst Bond Theme Ever.

After a couple of films featuring a comedy metal-toothed villain called Jaws, the series reached its nadir with *MOONRAKER*, which nowadays looks more like an Austin Powers movie than an Austin Powers movie does.

The series has never plumbed such depths since. Timothy Dalton's Milk-Tray Man portrayal was a bit dull, Pierce Brosnan was better than Connery (again) and Daniel Craig is the first film version who's almost like the bloke in the books. (But nicer. And less of a semi-rapist.)

THE
WORLD OF
SPORT

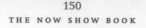

WORLD'S MOST EXCITING SPORT

This is tricky. All sport is actually the same sport, but with minor variations. This works roughly as follows:

Golf Ball must be hit into a small hole.

Hockey Ball must be hit into a net.

Football Ball must be kicked into a net.

Netball Ball must be thrown into a net.

Lacrosse Ball must be thrown into a net, from another net.

Basketball Ball must be thrown into a basket; but don't be fooled. It's actually a net.

Cricket Ball must knock sticks over. This takes practice, which takes place in a net.

Fishing No ball required – just the net. This is why it counts as a sport.

Rugby Proof that public schoolboys don't need namby-pamby nets – just sturdy poles. They're man enough to run and fetch the ball. And if they don't, they get detention. (In a net.)

Snooker Ball must be knocked into one of a series of *very small nets*.

You get the picture. The world's sports divide up into two basic types – ones that involve getting balls into or over nets, and those that don't. Those that don't include: downhill skiing, moto-cross, small-bore shooting, shot-putting, running and judo. The winner, though, and current holder of the title of world's most exciting sport, is obviously DARTS. Because where else can you see a bloke dressed in a pretend Dracula cape walking onto a stage and throwing small pointy things at a circle?

MOST LUDICROUS EXTREME SPORT

More and more people are trying their hand at extreme sports. People are jumping off bridges, jumping off cliffs, jumping out of aeroplanes, paragliding, parascending and driving like paramedics. Why? Because apparently you have to hang ten big style to the max if you want to touch the face of God, or something, and if you are a paramedic because you have to get to the accident quickly. Well, now, all these sports have a new rival from India, the officially recognised title-holder in this category – YAK SKIING (aka wilful lunacy involving yaks). Here's what happens:

A skier holding a bucket of nuts and facing uphill is attached to a rope which is passed through a pulley on a hilltop, and thence to a yak. The yak is below the pulley but near the top of the hill and the skier near the bottom. When ready, the skier then shakes his nut bucket loudly to attract the attention of the yak, which, infuriated at this invasion of his peace and

**solitude, then charges down the hill, yanking the skier
rapidly up the hill.**

OK, being pulled up a hill by an angry, hairy, two-horned ski-lift doesn't sound like much of a sport, still less an extreme one, but it apparently qualifies as such for two reasons. First, if the skier is particularly light or if the yak is particularly quick, the skier becomes no more than the stone in a catapult being hurtled uphill at great speed towards the mountain, an outcome with extreme consequences. Second, if the yak is coming down and the skier going up, the skier must inevitably meet the yak. By which time, the skier must have developed a pretty good reason why it has been deliberately irritating the great horny, Himalayan, hairy thing by rattling a nut bucket.*

*'Nut bucket' also being the slang term for a yak-skier.

MOST RIDICULOUS
OLYMPIC EVENT

By far the most ridiculous Olympic event takes place in the velodrome and is known as the KEIRIN. In it, a group of eight or nine cyclists chase down a pizza delivery boy on his moped until they catch him, eat his pizza, and leave him battered and bruised at the side of the track.

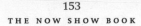

GREATEST MISSED OPPORTUNITY FOR NATIONAL PROMOTION

Now that the London Olympic Village is to be paid for entirely out of public money, there is a massive opportunity to give it a British theme. That is to make it as much like a British village as possible by giving it one bus a week, no Post Office and the services of an Olympic Village idiot, that being the person who told us the funding would be no problem in the first place, Tessa Jowell, or better still, Boris Johnson.

LEAST KNOWLEDGEABLE SPORTING CROWDS

The more high profile a sports event is, the less knowledgeable the spectators will be. Ryman League Second Division football is played in front of passionate groups of supporters who know every player and follow every match. World Cup finals are played in front of groups of executives from Mastercard and Pepsi who have no idea who's playing or, occasionally, which sport it is.

The dreaded Corporate Hospitality Packages dominate all really high-level sport, and pretty much every big event in the British sporting calendar is infested by investment bankers and management consultants getting all the best seats but rarely sitting in them. The worst examples are:

BRITISH GRAND PRIX A fair portion of spectators at the hugely expensive Bernie Ecclestone Experience don't watch any of the race at all. To be fair, Formula One is bemusing to watch and hard to follow when you're there; it's also deafeningly noisy. Fortunately, there will be a big screen in your corporate-hospitality tent, so you can watch the race on TV while never straying far from the buffet.

ASCOT No one at Ascot knows anything about horse-racing at all, apart from the Queen. In fact, the Queen probably wanders round Ascot muttering, 'Where were you lot for the 3.30 at Fontwell Park on a cold March afternoon, eh? Nowhere, that's where. Bloody part-timers. Why don't you all naff orf?'

WIMBLEDON I know about this one – I've been there. I've been a BBC guest on Centre Court, and I sat in the corporate area and was able to observe the goings-on. A man in front of me sat reading and texting on his BlackBerry through an entire set of Rafael Nadal; he then left. Another group of Pimms-swilling men in suits held a long discussion trying to identify one of the female players. (It was, er, Venus Williams.) Then, finally, half an hour into another match, a woman turned to her friend and said loudly, 'No, no – Federer's the one in the hat.' And these people had *Centre Court tickets*. It's enough to make you want to storm the Bastille.

MOST DISLIKED FOOTBALL CLUBS

All football clubs are disliked by supporters of other football clubs. The outsiders' image of other clubs generally runs as follows:

CHELSEA A rich man's plaything, the pampered playboys of the King's Road sold out to an even more pampered playboy who now hires and fires world-class managers at will in order to try and genetically engineer Chelsea into the new Real Madrid. This hasn't really worked, not least because the old Real Madrid are more a Greatest Hits album than a football team. The second-easiest club to hate.

LIVERPOOL Perpetually hankering after the glory days of 30 years ago, the Reds live constantly in the shadow of the other Reds just along the M62. Lacking the consistency and killer instinct of Man U, Liverpool possess one overwhelming asset – an ability to keep hold of players with Scouse accents so thick you need subtitles. This lends them a credibility way above most other Premier League sides, whose post-match interviews sound like a mashed-up Berlitz language tape. (Although Chelsea always keep a few Cockney hard men in the side, for old times' sake.)

MANCHESTER UNITED Enormously successful, determined, resilient and with a huge squad of players; therefore easy to understand why they are by far the easiest club to hate. It doesn't help that they are also the easiest club to like – the football club of choice for people who don't like football, in the same way that their fellow Mancs Simply Red are music for people who don't like music, or Jeffrey Archer is books for people who don't like books. This, however, is unfair on proper Man U fans who have watched the corporate mentality saddle the club with huge debts; sadly the corporate boxes were the first to empty when the credit crunch hit. They have been hoist with their own fatcat petard and as usual, it's the ordinary fans who are paying for it. All of which goes down very well with fans of other clubs, all of whom hate Man U.

NEWCASTLE The comedy club. Newcastle's famously loyal fans are renowned for their ludicrously high expectations. 'We are potentially a top-four club' they would say every season, before sliding into the relegation zone, and finally into the Championship and then back up again. Failure is invariably blamed on southerners; we may have 'kicked racism out of football', but if regional bias counted as racism, St James's Park would be almost empty on a Saturday afternoon. The Geordies loathe 'Cockneys', reserving their love for emotionally unstable bottler Kevin Keegan, who despite being manifestly unsuited for football management is still inexplicably regarded as a hero on Tyneside. If Sir Alex F. gave up as easily as Keegan does, he'd have walked out of Man U in 1987.

ASTON VILLA Mid-table plodders whose kit looks a bit like West Ham's, Villa have that 'there from the beginning' feel of a really old club who used to play in knickerbockers against Woolwich Arsenal and Accrington Stanley. They enjoyed a brief resurgence recently, before being upstaged by Man City, who were handed eighteen billion trillion pounds of oil-money and a little card that said 'Do Not Pass Go. Go Straight to Champions League.' Fortunately, it didn't work. If it had, football as a meaningful sport would have ceased to exist.

TOTTENHAM HOTSPUR Anti-Spurs chants are characterised by anti-semitism, which is misleading; Spurs are actually characterised by their rivalry with Arsenal. If you consult your A–Z you will see that Arsenal are based in a posher part of north London than Spurs. Arsenal also play in a bland corporate glass doughnut named after an airline, whereas Spurs still use four big sheds round the touchline and make you piss in a gutter. This, plus old-skool manager Harry 'I had no idea what was going to happen to Portsmouth' Redknapp, got them to the Champions League above Man City. So there's hope.

ARSENAL One of the few Premier League sides not to fire their manager every three weeks, Arsenal possess one of football's most articulate and philosophical managers and, at their best, can play beautiful flowing football that ranks alongside the finest in the world. Sadly, they don't do this quite often enough and their big corporate glass doughnut of a stadium is often rather quiet. Their season tickets cost over half a million pounds (good value compared with Chelsea) and many of their fans live in Islington, so the lack of atmosphere is often due to supporters texting their investment bank to see if they still have a job. Hard to really hate, unless you're a Spurs fan.

FULHAM Trailblazers in the 'rich foreign owner' stakes, Fulham were long owned by Di-and-Dodi conspiracy theorist Mohamed Al Fayed. Their ground covers a Thames-side spot overlooking picturesque Putney, and is thus possibly the most valuable piece of real estate in the Premier League. (Chelsea are stuck in an unprepossessing corridor between a cemetery and the District Line.) You'd have to say it's only a matter of time until Craven Cottage is replaced by Craven Executive Apartments, while the club move to a big plastic shed somewhere. Again, tricky to hate.

PORTSMOUTH Pompey fans are famous throughout the League for a) turning up and b) making a lot of noise supporting the team, rather than sitting in corporate seats texting their bank. Sadly, this fanatical following (including a man who turns up topless, painted blue and banging a drum) failed to stop a period of calamitous financial chicanery which has resulted in Pompey possibly changing their name to 'Southern Rock'. Only without the bailout. Almost impossible to hate, unless you're from Southampton, in which case you will have been played subliminal 'We Hate Pompey' tapes while still in the womb.

MOST PREMIERSHIP FOOTBALLERS SLEPT WITH

There are two records held in this category. The first is Most Premiership Footballers Slept With over the course of a lifetime (or 'career' if you are a topless model or WAG) and the second is for Most Premiership Footballers Slept With In One Night. Interestingly, the world record for both goes to then-19-year-old MANDY TOWNSEND from Leeds, who clocked up an impressive 300 (so far) in the former category and a no less impressive 15 in the latter. This second record was attempted in a bedroom at The Holiday Inn Express in Harrogate where an undisclosed Premier League football team were staying after a meal in a nearby restaurant where Ms Townsend worked as a waitress.

Some weeks later, Ms Townsend sent some home-made 'glamour' shots to *Nuts* magazine, which eventually led to a Page

3 photoshoot for the *Sun* where she became known as Mandy T, whose incisive opinion on the war in Iraq (as documented by the newspaper) was as follows:

> **Mandy T thinks the invasion of Iraq is undemocratic.**
> **She says, 'I want our boys to come home.'**

Over the next two years she became romantically involved with a number of footballers up to and around the 300 mark. During this period she spent an enormous amount of money on clothes, which is ironic considering she hardly ever wore any.

MOST CLICHÉS USED IN POST-MATCH INTERVIEW BY FOOTBALL MANAGER

In November 2008, immediately after a match between Nuneaton Town (formerly Nuneaton Borough) and Dunstable in British Gas Midland Division One, a football manager used a whopping 9,860 footballing clichés in just one short 2-minute interview. Anyone watching would have learned practically nothing of the game, apart from that 'the boys done good', 'they covered every blade of grass on the pitch' and that it 'was a game of two halves'. There was a glimpse into something resembling originality when we learned that Jamie Williams scored in the 16th and 57th minutes, but then this was undermined by the reason for those goals being that 'he gave 110 per cent'. Other footballing chestnuts trotted out during this interview included 'sick as a parrot', 'over the moon', 'there are no easy games', 'all to play for' and 'at the end of the day, Brian, football is a funny old game'. This one was especially noticeable, as there was no one called Brian there.

The interview was brought to a sudden, unexpected yet not entirely unwelcome conclusion when the local TV reporter who was conducting it screamed, on behalf of football fans and viewers everywhere, 'Shut up, you yawnsome, boring, unoriginal, sheepskin clad twunt' directly into the manager's face.

BEST BET FOR
NEXT MANAGER OF
CHELSEA FOOTBALL CLUB

Roman Abramovich has not yet found a manager who can deliver the success he craves at Chelsea Football Club. Various options have been tried −Ranieri, Mourinho, Scolari, Hiddink and current incumbent Ancelotti − and yet despite being among the world's best football managers all have so far fallen short.

If Abramovich wants a winner there is really only one man to whom he can now turn. A man who always wins, a man who has not lost for nearly 30 years: Robert Mugabe.

LARGEST PITCH INVASION

Pitch invasions usually occur during, or at the end of, sporting fixtures when the crowd wishes to celebrate or protest about an incident. Famously at the 1966 World Cup Final, Kenneth Wolstenhome was heard to report that 'some of the crowd are on the pitch' because 'they think it's all over', although it is now known Wolstenhome was wrong, as the real reason that some of the crowd were on the pitch was because there was a wasp in the stands.

Mass crowd rushes have happened worldwide for many years: on the 1971 Rugby Union Springbok tour (protests over Apartheid), a West Indies vs England Test Match (commentator Brian Johnston ran onto the pitch to hold the bowler's willy) and at the Australian Rules Football final in 1996 (the bar had just opened). However, the largest ever pitch invasion was in 2003, when the United States of America sent troops into Aston Villa because they'd heard there was oil under Villa Park.

Just after half-time, as the home team were 1–0 up against West Ham, the US Army deployed six Black Hawk helicopters 2nd Brigade (101st Airborne Division), a ground force of 200 Delta Force operatives backed up by 6,000 US Marines, 10 x HHC-1-504 PIR unmanned aerial assault drones, a mechanised infantry division of M1 Abrams battle tanks and an unspecified number of tactical air-to-ground missiles. The then President George W. Bush had told the UN and the FA that the decision to invade Villa Park was based on evidence that the premiership team were harbouring weapons of mass destruction, but none was ever found. At this point, the reason for the invasion was given as regime change, and as a result the then Aston Villa club manager

Graham Taylor was captured hiding in a hole and then hanged. At time of writing, seven years later, the American Armed Forces are still inside Villa Park, with no clear exit strategy.

SPORT YOU LEAST WANT YOUR CHILD TO BE GOOD AT

SWIMMING: A talented junior swimmer in the family is something to dread. Training for all swimming events takes place in cold, unfriendly swimming pools at 5 in the morning, and attendance is compulsory for all seven days of the week. This applies even if you live nowhere near the swimming pool in which the training takes place, and you therefore have to leave at 4 in the morning to get there. Once there, your child will plough endlessly up and down the pool for two hours while expecting you to watch, which is in fact pretty much all there is to do anyway other than eating Wagon Wheels from the machine or idling away the time wondering whether it is possible to get a verruca even if you keep your shoes on.

At the end of it all is the possibility not of untold wealth and fame, but an Olympic medal and a few appearances on the telly. Swimmers don't get the money or the celebrity of footballers, tennis players or even golfers. If you're really lucky, they might get an advertising deal of some sort, so your reward for years of sleepless nights and worry will be whatever you can get on eBay for the medal, plus the chance to see a poster of your offspring wearing branded goggles every time you visit a swimming pool. Which you never will again.

⚽

NB: Rugby runs swimming a close second – especially if your child is a girl. This has nothing to do with the game itself – it is exciting, and great to watch – it has to do with the fact that while 20 years ago rugby players looked like ordinary humans, they now have to be muscle-bound freaks who could crush you with their thumbs. Fortunately, not many rugby players have thumbs, at least not opposable ones. So, to avoid the freak child, discourage rugby.

(See *MUSICAL INSTRUMENT YOU LEAST WANT YOUR CHILD TO LEARN*.)

WEIRDEST SPORTING POINTS SYSTEM

The weirdest points system in modern mass participation sport is that of TENNIS, which sounds like it was invented by a genial Victorian drunk.

'Right, you play first and if you win the shot you can have 15. I don't know why. Then we can play again and if you win you can have another 15, so that's 30. And then you can have another 15 so that's 40, no hang on, it isn't. What would that be? Wait a minute, oh never mind, it's close enough. Then if I get 40 as well we will call that, what? Deuce. Yes deuce. I don't know why again. And if neither of us have anything we will call that love. Love all. Because, well, because I love you. I hope you're writing this down because there is no way I am going to be able to remember it in the morning.'

MOST DISAPPOINTING SPORTING PRIZE

Of the four majors in golf (US Open, British Open, US PGA and US Masters) it is generally accepted that THE MASTERS is the most coveted. For victory, the winner receives a small plastic-looking trophy and a Green Jacket, and with them the chance to look like a fresh produce manager from Morrisons who has won the staff incentive scheme.

MOST MISLEADINGLY NAMED OLYMPIC EVENT

The MODERN PENTATHLON consists of pistol shooting, épée fencing, show jumping, swimming and a cross-country run – and is, therefore, the most misleading of all Olympic sports as these particular events make it about as modern as the Ottoman Empire, crumpets and lemon curd. An attempt is being made to resolve this for the 2012 Games with five new disciplines being considered, among them Zorbing*, jet-surfing and killing a mutant android with a laser.

*Zorbing – a modern sport in which you roll down a hill in a miniature version of the Eden Project.

TELEPHONE-THROWING

The current world record-holders in telephone-throwing are:

Fixed line: RUSSELL CROWE (3m 52cm, at hotel employee)

Mobile: NAOMI CAMPBELL (2m 79cm, at own employee)

(The guy who threw the shoe at George Bush didn't know the difference between a shoe and a phone, so failed to enter.)

TRAVEL
AND
TRANSPORT

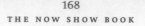

MOST USEFUL FLIGHT NUMBER INFORMATION

The first part of any flight number usually signifies the airline involved – for example, AA is American Airlines, LH is Lufthansa, and AL is Alitalia – while the number following it signifies that flight's position within that airline's schedule. It is rumoured, however, that the number following the British Airways call sign (BA) provides extra information and is an estimate of the number of bags that will be lost on that flight.

> **BA 1106 to Washington: 1,106 of the bags checked in will go to Baltimore, Frankfurt or outer space.**

To be fair, BA has recently reduced the number of bags lost. Sadly, this doesn't seem to be down to improved efficiency but simply because the ash cloud and industrial action have stopped them flying anywhere.

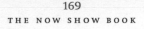

MOST GOLD, HOOPED EARRINGS SPORTED BY A SINGLE FEMALE 16-YEAR-OLD CHAV AS SEEN BY JON THROUGH A TRAIN WINDOW AS IT PASSED THROUGH CHATHAM IN KENT

167 (add another 40 if including her baby)

MOST TERRIFYING WORDS

The three most terrifying words in the English language are REPLACEMENT BUS SERVICE.

MOST OVERRATED TOURIST ATTRACTIONS

This depends on many factors, chief of which is how middle class you are. If the idea of Disneyland fills you with horror then you are utterly middle class. If it fills you with horror but you're going anyway, you are middle class but have children. Children can force people to do very odd things, like fly 3,000 miles across the Atlantic to visit a glorified funfair in which a giant trademarked mouse walks around under the delusion that modern children know who he is.

This is a highly controversial category which invariably prompts passionate argument, but the most generally agreed Over-Rated Tourist Attractions are:

MADAME TUSSAUDS, LONDON The National Portrait Gallery for idiots. You could understand it in the Victorian age, but quite why the 21st-century public flocks to see wax dummies of famous people, when the same famous people are appearing in every newspaper, glossy magazine, TV show and bookshop in the country, no one knows. It's not like you don't know what they look like. Although you do generally know that whatever they look like, it's not like the version at Madame Tussauds. So it's like a tribute band, but without the music. Or the band. Or anything.

THE GIANT'S CAUSEWAY, NORTHERN IRELAND For a long time the Giant's Causeway held a legendary quality because no tourists ever went to Northern Ireland, for obvious reasons. Then came the Good Friday Agreement and, after a slow and tortuous peace process, the good people of Ulster finally – after decades of civil strife – saw an end to violence and a return to normality for their troubled province.

The downside to this was that people actually started going to the Giant's Causeway instead of just hearing about it. When they got there, they realised that it's some volcanic rocks that have solidified in hexagonal columns. As a geology field trip, it's the business. As a tourist destination, it's about as exciting as basalt rock formations generally are to non-geologists. In the immortal words of Dr Johnson – 'worth seeing – but not worth going to see'. That quote, of course, has always really irritated the Northern Ireland Tourist Board, who often pretend that Johnson was actually talking about Buckingham Palace, which itself nearly made the list because it's a very dull building indeed. The only reason people look at it is in case Prince Philip pulls back one of the net curtains to moon at some foreigners.

LAND'S END, ENGLAND Yes, it is the most westerly point on mainland Britain but, ultimately, it's just some coast. It's a sticky-out bit of coast. Go to a nice beach instead.

DUBAI All of it. Hideous. (See *STUPIDEST-SHAPED ISLAND OFF THE COAST OF DUBAI.*)

LEAST RELIGIOUS NATION

Officially, the answer is CHINA, whose citizens are only allowed to worship large-scale engineering projects. (The Chinese government monitors all outgoing prayers and blocks them using a special firewall.)

However, Britain is also not a particularly religious nation, judging by a customer survey carried out by supermarket Somerfield in 2007. It was meant to test public knowledge **on the meaning of Easter*** and among the questions was:

'Why do we have an Easter bunny?'

And there were multiple-choice answers. Answer A was:

'Because he led the disciples to the place where Jesus was resurrected.'

Which Dan Brown apparently thought was the correct answer.

**It wasn't really to do any such thing, of course; it was to sell Easter eggs.*

Even better was the next question:

'Why do we give each other Easter eggs?'

To which answer A was:

'Because Jesus liked chocolate.'

The whole thing demonstrated perfectly the art of multiple-choice questionnaires (see *EXAM, EASIEST*), in that only a brainless dolt would not have given exactly the answers the client wanted.

WORLD'S LONGEST RAILWAY JOURNEY

The record for the world's longest railway journey is not held, as you might think, by Russia's Trans-Siberian Express, nor the Qinghai–Tibet Railway in China, nor the India-Pacific route from ocean to ocean across the bleached deserts of Australia. The record for the world's longest rail journey is in fact held by a commute on the 08.34 from Faversham in Kent to London, Victoria on Thursday 9 April 2009, a journey so slow that the actual *building* of the Trans-Siberian Express seemed speedy by comparison.

This may seem surprising, but in fact any train user worth his or her salt should not be surprised by this record, as in the UK train travel was ever thus. Cast your mind back to 1825 and the inaugural journey of the Stockton to Darlington railway. It was a triumph of mechanised steam, a revolution in transport and a new era in locomotion, and on opening day there was tension and the smell of the North in the air. The crowd fell silent as the great industrial visionary George Stephenson stepped forward to speak.

'We apologise for the delay,' he said, 'but the Stockton to Darlington railway is suspended due to overrunning engineering works. There is a replacement bus service in operation this morning between Stockton and Darlington. Or at least there will be, just as soon as someone invents a bus.'

And so it began. In those days it took two hours to travel 26 miles, roughly half what it takes now to cover half that distance on Southeastern trains.

On the morning of 9 April 2009 passengers were told, via the medium of unintelligible tannoy that is for some reason peculiar only to trains and stations, that the train would be delayed due to an 'incident' on the line at Gillingham. The incident turned out not to be an incident at all but rather an old armchair that someone had dumped next to the tracks, and the train ground to a halt until – and I kid you not – a police helicopter arrived and two policemen got out and moved it. That took two hours. Granted, it wasn't Southeastern's fault *per se*, but one has to wonder what happened to the pioneering spirit of the railroad. Where was the soul of the early founders of the Old West who dynamited their way across desert, rock and river to carry the brave new future of transportation across the new world?

And why is it that all of this human achievement, strength of character and resolve is now embodied in the shape of a slack-eyed Southeastern rail employee in a hat that's too big for him demanding you pay £35 for a ticket, despite the fact that the train you're both on can't even get from Canterbury to Victoria in under three hours without being held up by a comfy chair? I ask you this: would Casey Jones, rider of the Iron Horse and brave hero of the American rail frontier have waited for a helicopter to turn up and move a foam seat? No, he wouldn't. He'd have smashed straight through it because let's face it, in the battle between armchair and 382 tons of speeding metal, I'm fairly sure the latter would've won with ease. Casey Jones was hard. If a health and safety officer had tried to tell Casey Jones to stop for a chair, Casey Jones would simply have run him over. No wonder they once named a railway station burger outlet after Casey Jones. Casey Jones was no weedy vegetarian. Casey Jones would spit on a salad. And then run over it.

The journey from Kent to London is 60 miles long and is mostly through towns and fields, yet the train constantly stops, starts, stops again and terminates at stations that aren't even on the schedule. Recently, Jon went on a train journey from Salzburg to Klagenfurt in Austria. It's a journey of 130 miles through alpine tunnels, over glaciers, under lakes, above forests, over mountains, in and out of torrents of waterfalls and across ice bridges. And do you know what? This regular early morning train runs *to the second*, and the ticket costs just £7. And if there's an armchair in the way, it damn well goes over that too. Why is this? Why can their trains do that, yet ours can't even get across Kent without stopping because the line is covered in the wrong kind of furniture? I mean bloody hell, even Ivor the Engine ran to a tight timetable and he was a) a cartoon and b) had Welsh dragons living in his boiler.

Addendum: The second-longest train journey in the world finally arrived at its destination this morning. It began in 1981 when television's nylon freak show Jimmy Saville stood in front of an Intercity 125 and informed anyone within earshot that this was 'the age of the train'. The good news is that that very same Intercity 125 finally arrived in Manchester today after 27 years of being delayed just outside Crewe. Granted, the passengers all ate each other in about 1988 but hey, Casey Jones would be proud of that. JH

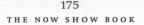

STUPIDEST-SHAPED ISLAND OFF THE COAST OF DUBAI

For some reason the Emirate of Dubai has become the coastline-du-jour off the end of which it is somehow fashionable to build any number of peculiar islands in any number of peculiar shapes. The first, and best known one, was the Palm in 2001: from the air a great fronded man-made structure in the shape of a palm tree, and to this day it's still full of half-finished houses mostly bought off plan by Premier League footballers or MPs looking to register it as their second home.

Dubai, of course, is the world's show-off. It's the international equivalent of the kid at school who always had to go one better. Largest shopping mall in the world? Check. Biggest amusement park in the world? Check. Most draconian laws that oppress women? Check. Death penalty for drinking a Lemsip? Check. World's tallest building? Check. (When it's completed, the Burj Dubai Tower is projected to be taller than Stephen Merchant.)

As Dubai continues to both laugh and wave its bare arse in the face of the credit crunch (even though bare arses are illegal), you can rest assured that there is no shortage of island-building plans. Currently under construction is an island the shape of each of Shakespeare's plays and, most stupid of all and thus holder of the current record, a man-made island in the shape of the saxophonist KENNY G. In December 2009 there was even a crazy notion that an island might eventually be built in the shape of a simple island, but this was laughed quite literally out of the water.

These increasingly bizarre land shapes serve no purpose except to demonstrate that the Sheikh of Dubai has got more money than sand. True story: when he wanted dolphins in the sea swimming round the bizzarro islands, he was told that the water was simply too warm for them and they would not survive. His solution? He refrigerated the sea. Seriously, he laid coolant pipes under the ocean floor and chilled the ocean to mammal-friendly temperature. Emperor Caligula would have been proud. (See ROYAL, MADDEST.)

MOST DESPERATE REGIONAL TOURIST SLOGAN

Britain is divided into many tourist areas. Some are obvious: Kent, where Jon Holmes lives*, is often known as the 'The Garden of England', because it is beautiful, well tended and, like a garden, we use it to store many of the things we don't really want any more, like bankers and stockbrokers.

Many areas attempt to attract tourists through their connection with great figures in British history. The area of the West Midlands around Stratford and Kenilworth is known, not surprisingly, as 'Shakespeare Country'. Likewise Coventry, claims at its railway station to be 'the City in Shakespeare Country', although that is largely because it sounds better than using its other great historical connection, which would demand the sign 'Coventry – The city Churchill knew was going to be bombed but said nothing – the bastard'.

South Tyneside prefers to be known by tourists as 'Catherine Cookson Country', the Yorkshire Moors near Middlesbrough as 'Captain Cook Country', while the Yorkshire Dales is abundant in alternative names – '*Heartbeat* Country', '*Last of the Summer*

---

*Note – Jon Holmes does not live, as is popularly believed, at the Bekonscot Model Village, near Beaconsfield. He did have a house there but sold it as it was too large.

Wine Country' and '*Brontë* Country', depending on whether the tourist board is targeting viewers of ITV, BBC1 or listeners to Radio 4. Channel 5 documentary viewers are, of course, encouraged to think of it as 'The Hills near Sutcliffe Country'. Elsewhere, Hampshire and Derbyshire both lay claim to 'Jane Austen Country', Dorset to 'Thomas Hardy Country', Cumbria to 'Wordsworth Country' and Cornwall, for want of anything else even remotely current, '*Poldark* Country'.

Yet while some areas have many historical connections to exploit, others are remarkably bereft, hence the title Most Desperate Regional Tourism Slogan goes to that flat, sodden section of Lincolnshire and the Fens known as HEREWARD THE WAKE COUNTRY. No, I didn't know either. He was the English King who led resistance against William the Conqueror. Quite.

MOST BICYCLES LOST BY A POLITICIAN

This title currently goes to cycling-crazy, flop-haired Tory *Prime Minister* DAVID CAMERON, who seems on average to have a bike stolen every six to nine months. You can understand the attraction for thieves. Cameron's are the only bikes that come with a chauffeur-driven car following 100 yards behind them.

Although his turnover of bikes is unhappily rapid – *this may be the real reason he has decided to walk to Parliament* – he has only ever appealed for the return of one, taken from outside a Ladbroke Grove supermarket in which he had been shopping – explaining that he thought of the bike as an 'old friend'. Presumably he also has an old friend he thinks of as a bit of a bike. I'll say no more.

MOST SLIGHTLY-ICKY
TRAIN SIGNAGE

In the toilet compartment of a mainline train, there's always a little notice that says 'Do Not Flush While Train is Standing in Station'.

Fair enough – until you think about it for a second. Does this mean that *everywhere else on the national track network is covered in raw sewage*? And what about when the train is going *through* a station? If you're in the loo on the London to York express, and the train is thundering along at 100mph through some little halt somewhere in rural Lincolnshire, do passengers waiting for the local train get showered with poo? No wonder it says 'Do Not Stand Near the Edge of the Platform'. What it should say is 'Stand Well Back or You'll Get Covered in Piss'.

STUPIDEST TOURIST COMPLAINT

The Association of British Travel Agents and Thomas Cook recently published a list of genuine complaints they've had from holidaymakers on their return. They paint a truly fascinating picture of the British abroad. Whinges included:

> **'I think it should be explained in the brochure that the local store does not sell proper biscuits like custard creams or ginger nuts.'**

The brilliant thing here is the whole concept of a *proper biscuit*. Foreign biscuits are obviously a leap in the dark, but it's often a leap worth taking. Those French bikkies with chocolate on are delicious. Custard creams, on the other hand, should never be eaten by anyone under 60, or who isn't called Doris.

Also, can you imagine how big holiday brochures would have to be if they included every piece of trivial information that a xenophobic idiot wants to know? The blurb under every villa and apartment would have to say 'there is a supermarket just half-a-kilometre away. The person on the till is Spanish, but the cost comes up on the till display, so you don't need to talk to them. They speak English anyway, but you'd only make fun of their accent as you waddle away with your cheap lager and custard creams.'

Another person complained that:

> 'No one told us there would be fish in the sea. The children were startled.'

Well, don't worry – if the EU's fishing lobby gets its way, that's not something you'll have to worry about for much longer. It is, of course, a bit of a shock when you stick your face into the Mediterranean and see fish, but that's only because nobody goes in the sea in Britain – it's too cold. Believe it or not, there are fish here, too, but your teeth are chattering too much to focus properly. Even so, the idea that someone should have to *tell you* that there are fish in the sea is a novel one. If these sorts of morons carry on complaining, then holiday beaches will be ruined by big Health and Safety signs reading 'Caution: Sea May Contain Fish'. Then perhaps people will be happy.

Another complainant wrote that:

> 'We bought Ray-Ban sunglasses for 3.50 from a street vendor, only to find out they were fake.'

That was from the chairman of the Financial Services Authority.

Then there was the woman who wrote that:

> 'Topless sunbathing on the beach should be banned. The
> holiday was ruined as my husband spent all day looking at
> other women.'

Frustrating and annoying for any woman, no doubt, but whether
Thomas Cook have the power to persuade other governments
to change the law on public beaches is somewhat doubtful. But
these are all understandable complaints of a sort. There were
others on a dumbness frequency that's almost surreal:

> 'It took us nine hours to fly home from Jamaica to England.
> It only took the Americans three hours to get home.'

Never underestimate how geographically ignorant people can
be. I once sat in a plane flying from Gatwick to Majorca, and
when we flew over some mountains, the man behind me turned
to his son and said 'Look – the Alps!' I nearly turned round and
said, 'How can they be the Alps? When we're flying south-west?
They're obviously the Pyrenees, you great twonk. Haven't you
ever looked at a map of Europe?' But I didn't, because I'm too
well brought up. I did feel sorry for the child, though, who even
now is probably flying to Miami and wondering why he can't
see the Himalayas. Finally, and current holder of the World's
Stupidest Complaint in the tourist category was:

> 'We had to queue outside with no air conditioning.'

That may have come from Elton John. But probably not.

HARDIEST NATION

GREAT BRITAIN is a nation unfazed when others panic. While the rest of the world bought up facemasks and closed down entire cities to try to stop Swine Flu, the British sent each other text messages saying, 'It's OK – the doctor's given me some oinkment.'

MOST FAMOUS BRIDGE

The world's best-known bridges, in order, are as follows:

1 **The Golden Gate Bridge,** San Francisco. It isn't the longest, or the prettiest, or the most spectacular, but it is the most famous, thanks to the movies. We've all seen it in the movies. Which makes up for the fact that it's quite a dull bridge.

2 **The Bridge on the River Kwai** If the Americans can have the most famous bridge just because of the movies, then the Brits can claim this one. Architecturally fascinating for its use of wood and bamboo, it is the only major bridge to be built by Alec Guinness.

3 **London Bridge** Quite a small bridge named after the nearby railway station. According to the song, it is falling down. This is strenuously denied by the Mayor of London, but that's probably to avoid compensation claims.

4 **A Bridge Too Far** Girder bridge over the Rhine at Arnhem. Scene of military disaster in 1944, as part of General Montgomery's disastrous 'Market Garden' Operation. The

failure of this operation led to America taking over command for the last eight months of the war, which in turn led to the handover of Eastern Germany to the Russians, which in turn led to the Cold War and a 40-year nuclear standoff at ruinous expense. So Montgomery has a lot to answer for, really. Should have stuck with tanks and sand.

5   **The Wobbly Bridge** Its real name is the Millennium Bridge, and it connects the north bank of the Thames at St Paul's with the Tate Modern at Bankside. It will, however, always be known as the Wobbly Bridge. Hundreds of years from now tour guides will be explaining to bemused tourists why this is – 'this spectacular structure suffered from The Curse of the Millennium, which afflicted all projects built for the Millenium apart from the London Eye, and that's only because they changed its name to the London Eye just in time.' If they'd called the Millennium Dome the 02 Arena from the outset, they'd have saved themselves a lot of grief.

6   **The Forth Bridge** Not the road one, which is quite dull. (But then so is the Golden Gate. If the weather in Scotland was like the weather in San Francisco, then the Forth Road Bridge would be just as famous.) No, we're talking about the railway bridge, a magnificent Victorian structure which makes you proud to be British. (Unless you're Scottish. In which case you don't want to be British. Although you are.) But whatever your Anglo-Caledonian-Saxon-Pictish ancestry, it's a superb bridge. It's famous worldwide because of the Hitchcock movie *The 39 Steps*, in which Richard Hannay jumps out of a train on the Forth Bridge – something which couldn't happen nowadays. There would be an announcement saying, 'Customers are requested not to escape from spies on this service until it has come to a complete halt at the next station.' The Forth Bridge

is also responsible for the famous simile, 'it's like painting the Forth Bridge', which is often used to mean any situation which is cold, wet and involves a brush.

7   **Take Me To The Bridge** Shouted by James Brown, the late godfather of soul, as a signal to his band that they should get ready to play the middle bit. Not strictly speaking a bridge in the sense of the other bridges, but I haven't disambiguated recently.

8   **Millau Bridge** An unbelievably spectacular road bridge across a deep gorge in southern France, the Millau Bridge was opened in 2004. Incredulous British journalists asked how on earth planning permission had been gained for a bridge in such a picturesque setting, and the French spokesman replied that 'in a beautiful place, one must build a beautiful bridge'. This contrasts with the British spokesman, who said that 'in a beautiful place one must hold an interminable planning enquiry, and then build a bridge really cheaply so it falls to bits after 20 years'.

9   **Sydney Harbour Bridge** Seven years in construction, this was opened in 1932 in order to 'provide the city with somewhere for documentary film crews to shoot footage of'.

10 **Jeff Bridges** Don't be silly.

11 **Allington Bridge** A suspension bridge somewhere in England, over which a large space rocket has to pass in order to reach its launch site. This is very poor planning on behalf of the rocket builders really, and obviously the rocket falls off the bridge and into the river. Only fans of *Thunderbirds* have any idea what I'm talking about. It's one of the best episodes. Thunderbird 4's finest hour.

DULLEST MOTORWAY

All motorways are by definition quite dull, but the record holder is a tough call. Leading contenders include:

M1 Aesthetically, this one is very poor, unless you are the kind of person who says 'Look kids! Luton!' All 1960s concrete bridges and Prestons of Potto lorries, the M1 is a dull drive. But it does take you from London to Yorkshire, so it is at least a proper journey.

M2 The London to Dover road. Historically, this is the route of Chaucer's pilgrims – and today, of course, illegal immigrants heading the other way. Despite being a route of enormous economic importance, the motorway stops at a roundabout near Canterbury. To the enormous amusement of French lorry drivers, it doesn't actually reach the port it's designed to serve.

M3 London to Southampton. Quite dull, but handy for Thorpe Park and Legoland Windsor.* At Winchester, however, it takes you through Twyford Down, a famous beauty spot and scene of one of Britain's most famous road protests. There ought to be a big statue of a private security guard punching a hippy in the face, called 'The Fascist Pig of the South'.

M4 Takes you west out of London, past Bath and Bristol and over the Severn Bridge into Wales. Not really dull at all, apart from the endless bit round Reading, which – judging by the length of time it takes to pass it on the M4 – is roughly the size of Tokyo.

*The Queen's newest grandchild. No one knows who thought of the name.

M5 Or, the Brummie's Escape Route. Every summer the M5 swarms with caravans as Midlanders head for the West Country. At Bristol all the Londoners join from the M4 and from there to Exeter it's just one big carriageway of regional prejudice.

M6 A godawful marathon of a motorway, the M6 sprawls through Birmingham like a stream of 1960s' vomit. There was a brief period in the late sixties when everyone in Britain was so stoned that they let town planners put motorways right through cities, while the residents just stood there saying 'the cars are such groovy colours!' London got the Westway and Birmingham got Spaghetti Junction before everyone woke up in the 1970s and realised they had asthma and a continuous rumbling noise near their house. The M6 then heads north past Stoke, round Manchester, and up through the Lake District, dumping you at Carlisle, where the Scots obviously took one look and said 'away w'ye, You'll no be puttin' that ugly bloody motorway through the bonny Borders tae Glasgow'. Because that's how they speak, innit?

M8 Links tough, salt-of-the-earth Glasgow to effete, money-obsessed Edinburgh. Or so the British Dictionary of clichés tells me.

M10 A rubbish motorway. Its total length is shorter than Sir Fred Goodwin's front drive.

M11 An inexplicable junior motorway which links London to Stansted Airport, which pretends to be 'London Stansted' but is in fact miles from London, which explains why Ryanair use it. North of Stansted, the M11 heads to its ultimate destination – the middle of nowhere somewhere west of Cambridge. Beyond that lies the no-man's-land of East Anglia, where road maps to this day just contain a blank space and the words 'Here Be Dragons'.

M40 A sneaky little motorway that doesn't go to lots of places. It doesn't go to Oxford, then avoids Abingdon, skirts round Warwick, misses Coventry and peters out in embarrassment.

M62 The Trans-Pennine motorway. Liverpool, Manchester, Huddersfield, Leeds, Hull. The signs are a sort of road version of *Final Score*.

However, the generally accepted record at the moment is held by:

M25 Officially the London Orbital Motorway, the M25 is the dullest road in Britain. Designed to help drivers avoid London (because London is interesting), it helps them skirt round it by taking a route which skilfully combines Green Belt beauty spots (which it ruined) and incredibly dull commuter towns (which were ruined already).

The M25 was built in the British way, i.e. by trying to cut costs as much as possible and thereby making it far more expensive in the end. The Department of Transport (see MOST INCOMPETENT GOVERNMENT DEPARTMENTS) asked road experts to predict traffic levels, and then completely ignored what they said. They predicted, quite correctly, that the M25 would not just re-route existing traffic round London, but would create a lot of new traffic of its own. Because of this, they recommended building it with three lanes and not many junctions.

The Department of Transport built it with two lanes and lots of junctions and, almost as soon as it opened, it was so overcrowded that it jammed solid. It had to be widened almost immediately (at great expense) and is now being widened again

.... ◌ೕ ....

(at even greater expense). Large chunks of the southern section also had to be resurfaced (at great expense) because they were built of cheap concrete and fell to bits. The people responsible for this massive waste of taxpayers' money probably all got knighthoods and have probably retired to somewhere nowhere near the M25.

MOST POINTLESS
NATIONAL GOAL

Some forty years ago on 20 July 1969, at exactly 20:17 GMT the lunar module of Apollo 11 landed in the Sea of Tranquility. At 02:56 GMT the whole world watched as Neil Armstrong fluffed his lines, forgot an indefinite article and became the first human to step onto the lunar surface, thereby fulfilling the promise of President Kennedy that America would have a man on the moon by the end of the decade.* It was an incredible achievement that captured the global imagination. A mere six decades after the Wright brothers first achieved powered flight, the human race had not only broken the bounds of our own atmosphere, but had landed successfully on our barren atmosphere-free neighbour.

By 1972, when the Americans gave up and instead concentrated on Skylab, the whole thing had become a little boring – five more Apollo missions had landed and successfully returned to Earth, and we had discovered practically nothing of any use save that the moon is grey, which you could see by looking through a telescope; that the grey wasn't simply the skin

---

*But see CONSPIRACY THEORY, WORLD'S STUPIDEST.

of a really excellent cave-aged Gruyère; and that if you hit a golf ball there it would go a very long way, which Tiger Woods can do anyway even with the little problem of gravity. Although, on the plus side, from the technology developed by NASA during the period we have now got the roll-on deodorant, fogless ski-goggles and the sports bra.

Anyway, by the early 1970s it was all done, and frankly no one cared anymore. Only now the Russians are at it again. They have stated with great excitement that they will have A MAN ON THE MOON BY 2025 – just fifty-six years after the Americans. What is the point? How is that going to impress the world? They might as well announce that they are going to invent a steam engine by 2015, build an iron ship by the end of the decade, develop the Spinning Jennyvich, or discover penicillin. It has been done already. The moon is old hat, everyone has been there, even Wallace and Gromit, and even that was twenty years ago. There is nothing left to be discovered, although Wallace and Gromit did throw the scientific community into turmoil by discovering not only traces of cheese but huge lumps of it.

The Russians, however, claim that there is more to be done on the lunar surface, that they will build a moon base – again, done by Gerry Anderson in 1973 – and launch a mission to Mars from there by 2035. Again, there isn't much point – the Martians have been here on Earth since Captain Scarlet.

Surely there must be something else the Russians can aim at as they seek to restore their national pride in the post-Communist era – like building a decent car or developing a method of Polonium poisoning that won't be traced back to their secret service. But not the moon, please not the moon, we've had enough of 1970s nostalgia.

MOST INEXPLICABLE
TRAIN ANNOUNCEMENT

The tannoy announcements at railway stations are famously annoying, especially when they started referring to 'customers' rather than 'passengers', thereby stressing that you are nothing but an anonymous spreadsheet quantity, rather than someone enjoying the experience of travelling. Any regular user of our Victorian rail system will encounter certain announcements at very regular intervals. All of them are guaranteed to produce either stifled groans or Tourette's-like outbursts of violent abuse from long-suffering 'customers'. They include:

'Cancellation due to staff shortages'
Driver is too hungover/lazy/militant to turn up for work.

'Signal problems'
Ancient 1960s wiring has packed up, having been poorly maintained by private contractor. We're currently bodging it back together with duct tape.

'All services delayed due to a person under a train at Selhurst . . .'
This is possibly the worst announcement of all. It brings out the very worst in people during the Darwinian struggle that is the morning rush-hour. The cold crackle of the PA system announces that some poor individual, weighed down by burdens beyond normal understanding, has ended their life by hurling themselves under a moving mass of metal. And all anybody ever says is 'Oh, you selfish bastard!'

However, the two finest announcements I personally have heard
– in over thirty years of taking trains in and out of London –
are as follows:

**'We apologise for the late arrival of this service. This is due
to the train slipping on the line at Deepdene.'**
I heard this at Reigate station many years ago. It was a cold,
frosty morning – but have you ever heard of a train slipping?
What happens in Scandinavia, or Russia, or Canada? Do their
trains have special spiky wheels? Or was the train drunk?

**'We apologise for the cancellation of the 8.14 to London
Victoria. This train has failed.'**
An enigmatic and slightly frightening announcement, heard at
East Croydon station. It is totally unclear what it means. What
is a failed train? Has it failed in a merely mechanical sense, or is
this a train in some sort of metaphysical crisis? What constitutes
'failure' for a train? Is some suburban three-coach multiple
unit lying depressed in a siding somewhere, crushed by the
realisation that, no matter how hard it tries, it will never pull
the Eurostar to Brussels? SP

MOST BORINGEST CAR JOURNEY AS UNDERTAKEN BY JON

In the years between 1978 and 1983 I went, with my family,
on the same journey from Nuneaton in Warwickshire to go
camping in North Wales in a succession of cars owned by my
parents. Despite the distance not being that great (although to

my young self sitting in the back of a vomit-inducing French car, it seemed as insurmountable as the Antarctic must have seemed to Shackleton), the journey from the Midlands to just outside Barmouth was the Most Boringest Car Journey ever.

It holds this record despite the best efforts of my parents who invoked various games to pass the time including 'I-Spy', 'Let's See, Out Of You And Your Sister, Who Can Keep Quiet For The Longest' and 'Why Not Silently Count How Many Blue Cars You Can See?', to which the answer was always, 'None because I'm in the back seat surrounded by sleeping bags and pillows and am thus cocooned in some kind of soft, downy hell that only serves to make one feel sicker.'

In fact, the journey was sometimes alleviated by actually *being* car sick. Once, coming back from holiday, having unwisely imbibed a banana milkshake before setting off, the ten-year-old me implored Dad to stop the car only two miles down the road, where I was promptly sick over a dry stone wall, covering a perplexed sheep in bright yellow child-liquid. My nana insisted that sitting on newspaper would help. All I did was read the newspaper, thus making the situation worse. And, what's more, at the end of the journey the glum, ungrateful young me knew that we were all about to spend seven days in a tent together in the rain on a fake island, as if Dante had popped back later to add a subsequent eighth circle of hell to his representation and posit that it was made entirely of canvas.

That was somewhere around 1983. However, the Most Boringest Car Journey these days is any undertaken while listening to Radio 4's *Quote . . . Unquote*. JH

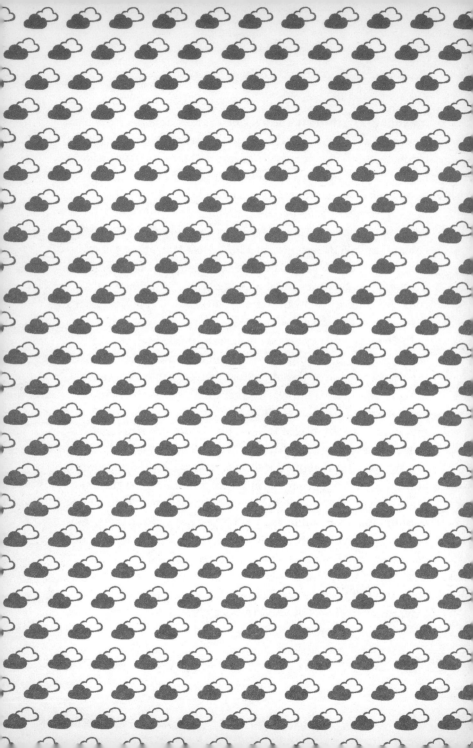

THE
NATURAL
WORLD

WORLD'S WEIRDEST PHOBIA

At the time of writing, the weirdest officially designated phobia* is undecided, but it's almost certainly one of these, in alphabetical order of freakiness:

ALEKTOROPHOBIA is the fear of chickens. Although, what with bird flu and everything, maybe this isn't quite as weird as it would have been a few years ago. Chickens themselves, of course, don't suffer from it. They tend to suffer more from Paxophobia,** which is a fear of having sage-and-onion stuffing rammed up their backside prior to one-and-a-half hours at Gas Mark 6.

BATHMOPHOBIA is the fear of stairs. Otherwise known as 'laziness'. Sadly, anyone who is afraid of stairs is likely to be even more afraid of lifts, which are much scarier.

CHRONOMENTROPHOBIA is the fear of clocks. You can always spot one, because they run screaming from the room during the opening titles of the *News at Ten*.

DISHABILIOPHOBIA is a fear of undressing in front of other people. This is a fairly common phobia, to be honest, although it will generally rule you out of a job at Spearmint Rhino. People who are definitely *not* dishabiliophobics include Paris Hilton, all Big Brother contestants under 25 and Kate Winslet (when working).

---

* All entirely genuine.   ** Except that one.

ERGOPHOBIA is the fear of work. There's a welcome upside to the credit crunch – ergophobics everywhere are experiencing the blessed relief that is compulsory redundancy.

FRANCOPHOBIA is a fear of the French, or of France. The real unfortunates are people who are alektorofrancophobic – they have a fear of French chickens. Their nightmare is a nice coq au vin.

GEPHYROPHOBIA is the fear of crossing bridges. This is quite a bizarre fear in this day and age – most modern bridges are really quite safe. All in all, a very strange phobia, unless, say, the bridge is somewhere in southern Afghanistan, and you're a British soldier, and you've spotted a wire coming from the bridge attached to a box with a big plunger sticking out of it. In which case, your gephyrophobia is to be commended.

HYPENGYOPHOBIA is the fear of responsibility. A surprisingly common fear nowadays thanks to compensation lawyers (see *MOST PARASITICAL AMORAL SCUM ON THE PLANET*) who have turned all teachers, doctors and anyone who deals with the public in any form into cowering wrecks. Teachers will sit and watch a child bleed to death rather than risk putting a plaster on them without appropriate supervision and/or written consent of the parent. Swimming teachers have it even worse. They can't jump in and rescue anyone as it involves touching an almost-undressed child, and that would make them a nonce. Now, the Health and Safety recommendation is that children are taught to swim in pools filled with polystyrene chips, since this allows them to take lessons fully clothed.

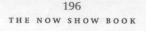

IATROPHOBIA is the fear of going to the doctor. Or, to be more precise, the fear of being told by a doctor that your minor twinge means you have three months to live. Most people suffer from this to some extent. In fact, anyone who doesn't is a bit weird.

JAPANOPHOBIA is a fear of the Japanese. Or, possibly, a fear of pretentious early-eighties New Romantic bands with a penchant for silly vocals and fretless bass.

KOINONIPHOBIA is a fear of rooms. Not to be confused with Llewelynbowenophobia, which is a fear of rooms totally buggered up by a TV makeover show.

LACHANOPHOBIA is a fear of vegetables. This is commonly suffered by small children, but may persist into adult life.

MELISSOPHOBIA/MOTTEPHOBIA These are related. Melissaphobia is the fear of bees, while Mottephobia is the fear of semi-retired football commentators.

NOVERCAPHOBIA is the fear of your mother-in-law. And that's a proper medical term, so Bernard Manning probably had a doctor's certificate all along.

OSTRACONOPHOBIA is the fear of shellfish. This is a very odd phobia. The sea has some terrifying things – sharks, stingrays, poisonous sea-urchins, deadly jellyfish – but shellfish? No. That's why Steven Spielberg made *Jaws* about a shark, and not a huge winkle.

PHALACROPHOBIA is fear of going bald. That's not really a phobia. That's a universal male condition.

PUPAPHOBIA is the fear of puppets. This is a terrible fear to have, as it is unlikely to be diagnosed in advance. Many parents are only aware that their child is pupaphobic when they take them to see Sooty in panto, and then notice a dreadful smell shortly after the star appears.

Q There are no phobias starting with Q, which may indicate that phobia-compilers are so terrified of the letter that they daren't use it.

RHABDOPHOBIA is a fear of severe punishment. Max Mosley was treated for this, with total success.

SIDERODROMOPHOBIA is the fear of trains. If the sight of trains terrifies you, then travel on Connex – you won't see one for hours. (That joke compulsory under the Obvious Gags Act 1989.)

TRICHOPATHOPHOBIA is, brilliantly, the fear of hair. It's very easy to scare a trichopathobic – show them a picture of Deep Purple in 1975.

UROPHOBIA is the fear of urine. Walking down any British high street at around 11.30pm on a Friday night should tell you if you suffer from this.

VENUSTRAPHOBIA is the fear of beautiful women. Seldom suffered from by footballers, oligarchs or rich businessmen, to the delight of divorce lawyers everywhere.

WALLOONOPHOBIA is the fear of Belgians. Very few people are scared of Belgians, and certainly not the German Army, which passed straight past them twice en route to France.

XENOGLOSSOPHOBIA is a fear of foreign languages. Suffered by most British schoolchildren, to the detriment of their employment prospects.

ZEMMIPHOBIA is fear of the great mole rat. No idea what that is, but it sounds pretty scary.

LEAST APPROPRIATE METHOD OF NAMING A WEATHER PHENOMENON

In 1953, it was decided by the American meteorologists that Atlantic hurricanes should have names, thereby making it easier for the general public to track their particular storm path. Six groups of names are rotated. For 2010 the names are as follows:

Alex Bonnie Colin Danielle Earl Fiona Gaston Hermine Igor Julia Karl Lisa Matthew Nicole Otto Paula Richard Shary Tomas Virginie Walter

But why? In 2008, there were Hurricane Arthur and Hurricane Bertha. What sort of crap names for wind are they? Arthur and Bertha? They sound less like hurricanes and more like senile elderly relatives. Although, to be fair, both are equally capable of causing hundreds of pounds worth of damage should they choose to visit your house.

Just look at the list. Who would bother to get out of the way of Hurricanes Danielle, Lisa or Julia? Tomas is a misspelt tank engine, not a whirling vortex of wind that takes the roof off your house. Colin sounds a hurricane that works on Saturdays in Curry's (see *ELECTRICAL RETAILER'S SO-CALLED GOLD WARRANTY, MOST POINTLESS*) and Gaston, the French hurricane, will probably go on strike anyway.

It is quite apparent that meteorologists name hurricanes with much less care and attention than celebrities employ when naming children. Bringing in a few pop stars and actors would possibly help. 'The Gulf Coast of America is being evacuated this morning ahead of the predicted landfall of Hurricane Fifi Trixibelle. This follows the widespread destruction caused last year when Peaches Geldof smashed into Louisiana and tore up trees and buildings with the force of an atomic bomb.' (See *POP STAR'S CHILD'S NAME, SILLIEST*.)

For clarity, however, hurricanes need to be scary, not Shary, and therefore need a new system of identification. We suggest that for 2011, they are named as follows:

- Apocalypse
- Brown trousers
- Crikey
- Destruction
- End of the World
- F**k me it's Windy
- Ghengis
- Help!
- Ivan the . . . aaaagh!
- Just Run
- Karadzic
- Look out Scoob!!!
- Merciless
- Nasty
- Oh Shit
- Panic
- Quick, to the . . . Basement
- Relentless
- Shipman
- Terror
- Uh Oh
- Vortex of Death

Another school of thought, interestingly, suggests that we should give hurricanes deliberately *unthreatening* names, in order psychologically to take away some of their power. You would be less frightened if you heard a news report that said, 'And this time round the residents of Brownville, Texas, are staying put, believing that Hurricane Bert will pose no more of a problem than Hurricane Ernie did this time last year.'

In 1983, the National Weather Center in the United States reported that the late Hurricane Higgins had got drunk again and smashed up Florida.

MOST NERVOUS
WEATHER FORECASTER

This record has stood for over 65 years and will possibly never be broken. It is held by GROUP CAPTAIN J.M. STAGG who, on the night of 5 June 1944, had to forecast the next day's weather to Dwight D. Eisenhower, the Supreme Commander of Allied Forces in Europe, Field-Marshal Montgomery and other top brass in charge of the D-Day invasion and the relief of the European mainland from Nazi tyranny. The whole thing hinged on whether the wind would have dropped by morning, and the whole occasion was quite unquestionably the Most Important Weather Forecast ever made.

Interestingly, at the same time, Michael Fish had been parachuted into Germany by Special Intelligence Ops and had made his way to Berlin, where he appeared on German radio, telling listeners that 'a woman phoned earlier today to say that she'd heard there was a massive Allied amphibious assault on the way. Well, don't worry – there isn't . . .'

FUNNIEST FISH

See *FINNIEST FISH*.

MOST NOTORIOUSLY IGNORED WEATHER FORECAST

In 2005, Hurricane Katrina was tracked by satellite from the mid-Atlantic across Cuba and into the Gulf of Mexico, where it headed for New Orleans. The entire world's media had been tracking its progress for a week as it headed inexorably for that great and historic city. Bizarrely, the only person who hadn't been tracking it was President George W. Bush who was playing golf. He reportedly asked Dick Cheney to 'find Michael Fish and check he's on the case'.

MOST INACCURATE WEATHER FORECAST

Ex-BBC weatherman MICHAEL FISH still holds this record, for his notorious forecast of OCTOBER 1987. However, whenever they show the famous clip, they always cut it off very sharply after he says:

> 'A woman phoned earlier today to say she'd heard there was a hurricane on its way. Well, don't worry – there isn't . . .'

...CHOP! They always cut it off right there. The reason for
this is that Fish goes on to say that there will be very high winds
in the south, and so wasn't actually that wrong at all. It isn't like
he said:

> '... don't worry – there isn't ... in fact, it's going to be a balmy,
> calm night with not a breath of wind, just a romantic moon
> beaming down from a cloudless sky.'

No. He just didn't predict an actual hurricane, which to a
meteorologist is a specific technical term. So it's about time we
let Fish off, really. Although we won't. He remains in the record
books as the World's Worst Weather Forecaster and will never
live it down.

MOST BORINGLY NAMED PLANET IN THE SOLAR SYSTEM

No contest – EARTH is the most boringly named planet in the
Solar System. No one knows why we have given all the other
planets interesting names except ours. It's like calling your
children Sacheverell, Dionysus, Thor and Clytemnestra, and then
calling yourself Colin.

The other planets have much cooler names:

Mercury is named after the Greek messenger who pedalled
frantically around the heavens delivering packages between the
other gods.

Venus is the Roman goddess of love.

Mars the god of war.

Neptune the god of the sea.

Jupiter the head of the gods.

Saturn God of agriculture. (Although growing conditions on Saturn are generally quite poor.)

Uranus God of *Carry On* films and innuendo.

Pluto Sorry. This planet is no longer available.

MOST COMEDY PETS

1 BUDGIE No one keeps budgies any more. Except mad old ladies or people who think keeping a small, brightly coloured tropical bird in a tiny cage in a cold Northern European country is nice for the children. The comedy attribute of the budgie is that it can supposedly be taught to speak, except it obviously can't. It just makes odd noises that sound a bit like speech, a bit like Julie Burchill.

2 FERRET Be honest. If someone kept ferrets, you'd think they were weird. You'd think they were living in some sort of Keith Waterhouse fantasy northern land, like *Last of the Summer Wine* with rodents.

3 PIGEONS There's a bit of a northern theme creeping in here. Apart from ferrets, comedy northerners used to keep homing pigeons. These are pigeons which get driven in a van to somewhere miles away and then fly their own way back. Every time they were loaded into the van they must have thought, 'Oh no, they're going to drive me miles away just so I can fly home again. It's not that clever, for God's sake.' Homing pigeons are not to be confused with racing pigeons, which are much more highly trained. Rather than just flying home, they fly at speed around a track, sometimes going over hurdles, and in the exciting 4-by-400-metre relay, carrying a little baton in their beak.

4. PITBULLS There is no excuse for owning a pitbull. Nobody needs one. They are just status symbols for a particular type of boneheaded chav male, whose idea of a pet is a vicious ugly dog that can kill things. Sadly, the things they kill are seldom their owners, but small children or relatives.

5. CORGIS These are comedy pets for one reason – they are the Royal pets. Of all the many animals that have been cross-bred from the wolf over the last few thousand years, the corgi is one of the most genetically embarrassing. Imagine being a wolf and trying to recognise the waddling low-slung Basil-Brush faced Queen-botherer as your own flesh and blood. It'd just be mortifying. Some dogs – Alsatians, Labradors, even some spaniels – have a sleek, proud nobility to them. Others just lie around Buckingham Palace like tubby little draught-excluders, waiting for a footman to feed them some more quail. Utterly pointless dogs, their only value is that they can be trained to sneak up on visiting Presidents and dignitaries, and piss on their legs when they're not looking.

SHALLOWEST LAKE

Up until 1975 the shallowest lake was either Lake Chad (in French, *Lac Tchad*) in Africa, which is only 10.5 metres (34 feet) at its deepest or, of the Great Lakes, Lake Erie on the North American/Canadian border with an average depth of 19 metres (62 feet) and a maximum depth of 64 metres (210 feet).

However, more recently, scientists using sophisticated measuring equipment have concluded that the shallowest lake in the world is actually GREG LAKE, largely due to his song 'I Believe In Father Christmas'. This song, ubiquitous in shopping centres worldwide from the middle of October onwards, has no measurable depth whatsoever and is considered to be 'dead', in that it contains way too much schmaltz to harbour life. Proof of this is to be found early on in the song* and Greg Lake is now considered a biological hazard and has been officially placed on the 'hazardous – do not listen' list by the Department of Agriculture, Fisheries and Mawkish Christmas Songs.

*The Now Show Book *didn't even bother to ask permission to quote this song as it is so wet that it would make the page you are holding all soggy. Instead, we recommend that you go and google the lyrics yourself, paying particular attention to the bit about the veil of tears for the Virgin's birth. But take wellingtons and a sou'wester.*

WORST MISTAKE OF DIVINE PROVIDENCE

God has made many big decisions down the years, among them how many days should he take to make the Earth, should the Sun be incandescent or low-voltage, and which would be more appealing, a land of milk and honey or a land of yoghurt and Nutella?

Frankly, though, many decisions have been a mite controversial. For example, many commentators remarked at the time that his decision to take only two of each species on the Ark, with no spares or substitutes, was an unreasonable risk and so it proved, resulting in the loss of several antediluvian animal species, and with that the revoking of God's membership of WWF, Greenpeace and the RSPCA. The greatest losses were perhaps the unicorn – the horse with a power drill on its head – the griffin and the mermaid, of which they brought two but then forgot to bring any mermen. (See *FUNNIEST CREATIONIST THEORY TO EXPLAIN AWAY AWKWARD FACT*.) Noah himself offered to help propagate the species, but Mrs Noah was having none of it, and neither was Noah once his wife found out what he was thinking.

Yet of all God's decisions, possibly the worst was to put the holiest places of three of the world's Abrahamic religions all within a few hundred miles of each other, that is, to make them all Abrahamic in the first place. Had he taken just a bit more care, and made the holy city of Christianity say, Ottawa, that of Judaism, Auckland, and that of Islam, Milton Keynes, I doubt there would have been any tension at all. Sadly, God missed this opportunity and put everything in the Middle East, where he then compounded his error by sticking the oil there as well. Well, there, and Russia, Venezuela, the coast of Louisiana (where it is still available free to anyone with a sponge and a bucket) and Antarctica, where, thanks to global warming caused by burning so much oil, we can now get at the oil which we were prevented from reaching by all that inconvenient ice. All of which can only lead to the conclusion that either God was having a bit of a laugh, or just isn't very good at the decision thing and we might all have been better off with Lord Alan Sugar in charge.

MOST AGGRESSIVE PRIMATE

Britain's most aggressive primate is Dr Rowan Williams.

WORLD'S LARGEST DISLOCATABLE JAW

The world's largest dislocatable jaw is often attributed to the Green Anaconda (*Eunectes murinus*). Anaconda snakes are startlingly large, being up to 35 feet long and 13 inches in girth. Their jaws, however, are not strictly dislocatable as the upper jaw does not form part of the skull as in humans but is fixed to it through tendons and ligaments, a system which allows them to open their jaws 150° and devour animals larger than themselves, having first subdued their prey through constriction and suffocation. The largest jaw dislocator in the strictest sense is the GORDON BROWN (*Primeminister nolongerusus*), who shares with the anaconda an ability to devour his prey whole having first rendered them unconscious by simply talking to them. However, under intense stress, the jaw of the GORDON BROWN may become uncontrollable and may involuntarily call innocent members of the public 'bigots', thus rendering itself unelectable.

MOST POINTLESS BITS OF THE HUMAN BODY

There are many useless bits of the human body – the coccyx (a vestigial tail once used for balance and mobility), wisdom teeth (third molars that early humans used to grind down plant tissue), and the appendix (the reference section found at the end of the digestive system). Each of these has now been rendered useless by the evolutionary path chosen by homo sapiens, although there is a remote possibility that they may regain some of their previous function amongst small groups of the population. For example, binge drinkers and others who suffer from dramatic and regular loss of balance may favour the gene permitting tail development.

Likewise, diners in poor vegetarian restaurants are likely to develop larger wisdom teeth. This process will of course take millions of years, just long enough for the waiting staff to deliver the starter.

In addition, other vestigial body parts are – the vomeronasal organ (a tiny pit either side of the septum – a body part itself considered dispensable by some *Heat* magazine regulars), male nipples (useless, but fun to have) and the sinuses – horrid mucus-filled air cavities in the cranial bones which are thought originally to have been lined with scent receptors, giving our ancestors a heightened sense of smell, although obviously mainly of mucus. It is now also thought that the air-filled holes of which the sinuses consist have the benefit of making the skull lighter, a trait thought to have developed through the early species intermingling of man and Malteser. Without sinuses, humans would therefore require either smaller heads or larger neck muscles to hold their heads up. In this sense, then, sinuses are far from useless, in that they stop us all from being immensely ugly.

MOST WORRYING THINGS THAT COULD HAPPEN TO PLANET EARTH (APART FROM GLOBAL WARMING)

Despite the fact that the global temperature seems to be spiralling out of control, our ice caps are melting faster than a Magnum in a sauna and the climate is changing in unexpected and potentially disastrous ways, there are other more catastrophic events for us all to worry about.

In fact, when seen in the context of the history of the planet as a whole, the period during which human life has developed has been extraordinarily benign geologically and atmospherically, with barely an orogeny, massive tectonic plate movement or cosmic collision to worry about. Human life is, therefore, fragile and dependent upon conditions which have only prevailed relatively recently, and which could easily disappear in a moment. Worrying, isn't it?

In fact, we are all under threat from a series of statistically pretty unlikely 'extinction-level events' or ELEs – at least that's what they were called in *Deep Impact* when we were saved by Morgan Freeman, which is an unlikely event in itself. As far as I know, the only impact he has ever actually dealt with was when his car crashed and he was found to be with a woman who wasn't his wife. Possibly there was then a second impact at the hands of his wife, I don't know. The most worrying of all ELEs is probably:

1 METEORITE STRIKE Particularly as a previous hit is thought to have wiped out the dinosaurs. A big enough meteorite could knock us out of orbit, put us further away from

the Sun and thereby reduce photosynthesis so much
that nothing could grow, but that isn't really the big worry.
No, the big worry is that a relatively small strike could produce
a cloud of dust so large that the Sun's rays would be blocked
out and thereby reduce photosynthesis so much that nothing
could grow. OK, the worries of a big strike and a small strike are
roughly the same, so probably it is just a strike, forget the size,
that we should worry about. But hey, don't get too low, there
are solutions to the problem. First, Bruce Willis already has
experience of being lowered onto a meteorite and blowing it
up before it gets near us, so we can just send him up there again
and, second, even if Bruce fails there remains a chance that the
meteorite might hit southern England where the sheer number
of children's trampolines will bounce it straight back into
deep space.

Other pant-wetting nightmares are:

2 SUPERVOLCANO Now, volcanoes we can cope with.
They spew ash and magma high into the atmosphere but
rarely threaten to block out the Sun's rays, thereby reducing
photosynthesis so much that nothing will grow – yes, it's that
old threat again – but a supervolcano, in other words a volcano
that makes Vesuvius look like a mere pimple easily dealt with
by Clearasil, that is a completely different matter. That could
block the Sun out, no problem. Oh, and don't panic now, but
there is one under Yellowstone National Park. It has erupted
three times in the last 2.1 million years, and it is due to erupt
again any time now. If that mother goes up, no one is going to
be tanning any more. Our best bet is either to build an enormous
cooker hood over Wyoming, or pray that the day the volcano
erupts an enormous meteorite lands in it and plugs the hole.

3 GAMMA-RAY BURST Again, this is a bit worrying because although it may only occur once or twice every thousand million years, it is a possible hypothesis for Earth's great Ordovician extinction 450 million years ago – the third largest of the five major extinction events in Earth's history. Basically, a ten-second burst of gamma radiation from a star 6,000 light years away could destroy half the ozone layer almost immediately, causing a massive drop in temperature and, guess what, the death of those species reliant on photosynthesis. Yes, it is photosynthesis again, sorry. Short of covering the whole planet in factor 30, there is stuff-all we can do about it, although you might want to think about buying a really thick winter coat and getting a few tins in. Some microwaveable food might also be a good idea – given the amount of radiation that would be flying about you wouldn't actually need the microwave, though.

4 MAGNETIC POLE REVERSAL At the moment, the Earth has the North Pole at the top and the South Pole at the bottom, but it hasn't always been like this. Well, it has, in that the top has always been the top and the bottom has stayed where it is, but the polarity of each has changed, as is shown by a study of iron crystals in rock. The Earth has flipped magnetically roughly once every 200,000 years, but here is the good thing: this is not a life-threatening event. It shouldn't even be in this list. You will be fine, the process won't kill you, unless on the day the polarity finally changes you are orienteering with a compass, the map tells you that there is a sheer 1,000-foot gorge to the north and you set off into the gathering darkness in the direction you think of as south.

5 SOLAR EXPANSION Now, I'm sorry about this, but this one will definitely happen. Unlike the others, it isn't an 'if', it's a 'when'. As the Sun runs out of the hydrogen which keeps it as a nice focused little ball of fire at the centre of the solar system, it will begin to expand until eventually it consumes all the planets around it. Now obviously, Mercury and Venus will get it before we do, but eventually the Earth will be flame-grilled, Joan-of-Arc style, as would we be if any of us were still left, which we won't be. The conditions required for life will have disappeared thousands, even hundreds of thousands of years before, as the oceans boil dry and the atmosphere burns off. Don't worry though because although it is going to happen, it is an awfully long way off, so far off in fact that by then small businesses may even be able to borrow money again. So not really even worth bothering about, frankly.

FINNIEST FISH

See *FUNNIEST FISH*.

MOST HEARTBREAKING PETS

Pets are useful for all sorts of things – companionship, loyalty, security, and a handy introduction to a whole range of worm-based diseases. They are principally useful, however, for introducing children to the idea of death, in all its forms. Accident, illness, old age – they all come with your little furry, scaly or finny friend.

·· ❮◀◀◀◀◀◀ ··

GOLDFISH Die on you regularly, often for no apparent reason. One morning you find them floating at the top of the tank like a little orange Mafia victim. If you keep them outside in a pond, it's even worse, because they sometimes just disappear, even more like a Mafia victim. Maybe that's the way to explain it to the kids. 'He got on the wrong side of Joey the Heron. Whaddya say? Bada-boom! Down the beak. That's the way it goes. Say nuthin' to no one.'

CATS In addition to diseases, cats are given to fighting with other cats, and will appear in the morning with bloodied patches of missing fur. If you tackle them about this they look at you as if to say 'He started it. He disrespected me, yeh?' and generally act as if you ought to mind your own business. Even worse, however, is that cats have a very poor grasp of basic road safety and, if you want to own one, you need to prepare your children for the moment when Tiddles gets hit by a car. They will perhaps assume that this will take the form of an amusing cartoon-style incident in which the cat will be temporarily flattened into a pancake-style cat with a single tyre mark running vertically down it (see THINGS THAT HAPPEN IN TOM AND JERRY), but that isn't actually what will happen. The cat will instead hide under the sofa, meowing piteously when you try to coax it out. You need to get it to the vet quickly, and it probably isn't worth buying it a return ticket.

RABBITS Nice pets. Friend of mine had one. They built a little hutch in the garden. One night a fox got into it. You might as well have put the rabbit into a food-processor and switched it on, frankly.

0 0 1 1 0 1 1 1 0 0 1 0 0 1 0 1 0
1 0 1 1 0 1 1 0 1 0 0 1 0 1 1 0 1
0 1 1 0 1 1 0 1 0 0 1 0 1 1 0 1 0
1 1 0 1 0 0 1 0 1 1 0 1 0 0 1 0 1
1 0 1 1 0 1 0 0 1 0 1 1 1 0 0 1 0
0 0 1 1 0 1 1 1 0 0 1 0 0 1 0 1 0
1 0 1 1 0 1 1 0 1 0 0 1 0 1 1 0
0 1 1 0 1 1 0 1 0 0 1 0 1 1 0 1 0
1 1 0 1 0 0 1 0 1 1 0 1 0 1 0 0 1 0
1 0 1 1 0 1 0 0 1 0 1 0 1 1 1 0 0 1 0
0 0 1 1 0 1 1 1 0 0 1 0 0 1 0 1 0
1 0 1 1 0 1 1 0 1 0 0 1 0 1 1 0 1
0 1 1 0 1 1 0 1 0 0 1 0 1 1 0 1 0
1 1 0 1 0 0 1 0 1 1 0 1 0 0 1 0 1
1 0 1 1 0 1 0 0 1 0 1 1 1 0 0 1 0
0 0 1 1 0 1 1 1 0 0 1 0 0 1 0 1 0
1 0 1 1 0 1 1 0 1 0 0 1 0 1 1 0
0 1 1 0 1 1 0 1 0 0 1 0 1 1 0 1 0
1 1 0 1 0 0 1 0 1 1 0 1 0 0 1 0
1 0 1 1 0 1 0 0 1 0 1 1 1 0 0 1 0
0 0 1 1 0 1 1 1 0 0 1 0 0 1 0 1 0
1 0 1 1 0 1 1 0 1 0 0 1 0 1 1 0 1
0 1 1 0 1 1 0 1 0 0 1 0 1 1 0 1 0
1 1 0 1 0 0 0 1 0 1 1 0 1 0 0 1 0 1
1 0 1 1 0 1 0 0 1 0 1 0 1 1 1 0 0 1 0

SCIENCE
AND
TECHNOLOGY

101001
010110
110001

MOST POINTLESS FONT

Wingdings. Or, as Wingdings would be written in Wingdings:

✧✹■♑♎✹■♑✦

TALLEST BUILDING

The tallest structure in the world this week is the PEANIS SUBSTITUT TOWER in Brunei, which took over from last week's tallest, the Staytus-Cimbell Building in Singapore, which took over from the previous tallest, the Me-Too Tower in Taipei. Sadly now out of this category is the Kredit-Krunch Tower, a half-completed pile of scaffolding half-a kilometre high. Work has also halted on the I.M.M.I.Grant-Labour Building in Dubai, a 200-storey hotel where every room comes with an underpaid foreigner finishing the grouting.

SOFTEST METAL

Up until comparatively recently, scientists have believed the softest metal to be caesium. Discovered spectroscopically in 1860 by Robert Bunsen and Gustav Kirchhoff, caesium is a soft, silvery-gold alkali metal which is liquid at room temperature. Extremely reactive, it finds limited use in vacuum tubes and in atomic clocks so accurate that they vary by no more than 5 seconds in ten generations. Caesium has the atomic number 55 and an atomic weight of 132.9054, while its electron configuration at ground state is 1s22s22p63s23p63d104s24p64d105s25p66s1.

However, since their groundbreaking 1986 album *Slippery When Wet*, the softest metal in the world is now thought to be BON JOVI.

POSHEST BIOFUEL

It is reported that at his Highgrove Estate in Gloucestershire, Prince Charles has converted his Aston Martin to run on a biofuel based on waste products from the manufacture of cheese and red wine.

Presumably the fuel comes in two grades:

Duchy Ultimate – Roquefort and St Julien Medoc (Premier Cru Classe. Appellation St Julien Controlée)

Duchy Standard – Beaujolais Nouveau and Dairylea Dunkers

MOST ACCURATE MODEL FOR GLOBAL WARMING

Under the auspices of the Intergovernmental Panel on Climate Change (IPCC) scientists concerned by the recession of the ice at the North and South Poles have spent the last few years developing sophisticated computer models to predict how fast these changes are happening and what their end point might be.

Much of this effort has centred on assessing the effect of fluid dynamics, radiative transfer and the positive feedback loop set in motion when ice which reflects incoming radiation is replaced by water which largely absorbs it. This differing climate sensitivity in the models has meant that the predicted temperature rise varies from 1.1 to 6.4∞ Celsius by the end of the 21st century, while newer studies continually find errors in the assumptions of their predecessors. So far, all models have failed to predict the rapidity of the shrinkage of Polar ice.

All that is, bar one. It is ironic, given the then pitiful power of computing, that the most accurate model for global warming so far seems to be that developed in the 1970s for FOX'S GLACIER MINTS, in which a single polar bear floats slowly southwards on the last remaining lump of ice, while being taunted by a fox, whose ability to stand habitat change is much greater.

MOST FAMOUS SCIENTIST

The world's most famous scientist is EINSTEIN, who wasn't really a scientist at all. He didn't do anything with test tubes or laboratories or anything. He just sat around thinking and writing equations. This left him lots of time to become a celebrity, one of the very few scientists to achieve genuine fame among the general public. By 1925 he had been featured in *OK!* magazine, under the headline 'Brainy Albert Shows Us Around His Fabulous Boffin's Hideaway', and had been interviewed by *Nuts*, where he gave his opinions on the 'Top 10 Relatively Busty Babes of the Year!'

STRONGEST MAN-MADE OBJECT

Not steel, not granite, not even Ross Kemp with his bald face pumped full of rock cakes made of titanium. Instead, the strongest object known to man is any kind of cable and/or electrical lead that's simply been left in a box for a while. You can test this yourself. Simply take an extension lead or a phono cable from your hi-fi and leave them together in a box. When you return, the resulting knot will be the envy of any Venture Scout you care to name. Mountaineers often use this technique as a foolproof method of not dying. Scaling Everest in 1953 Sir Edmund Hillary simply threw a four-way surge-protected 13-amp extension lead from B&Q over the side of the Southeast Ridge and by morning the resulting tangle was strong enough to hold him; Tenzing Norgay; eight Sherpas; all their equipment; Beth Ditto, lead singer of The Gossip; and 27 circus elephants the size of Wales. Plus 27 whales the size of circus elephants.

In engineering, the longest bridge held up using the tangled cable method is the Dartford Crossing on the M25. The cables suspending the bridge platform 137 metres above the River Thames are actually some old Christmas tree lights that were put away in the attic without coiling them properly.

MOST RIDICULOUS BRITISH MILITARY HARDWARE

The record in this category is quite uncontested. The most ridiculous British military hardware is the BLUE PEACOCK NUCLEAR MINE, which was built in the 1950s and tested (although not exploded) in Kent. The idea was to build an atomic bomb that would be left buried in the ground in West Germany. If the Russians invaded we would wait a few days and then set it off remotely, thus nuking them Russkies in a sneaky way.

So far, so Cold War paranoia. What elevates the Blue Peacock into the record books is that there was a problem with it. The problem with it was, that in winter it got too cold underground for the electrical circuitry to work, and it wouldn't go off. Various solutions were proposed for this. One of these solutions was that the bomb should be buried *with a live chicken inside it*. The chicken would be given a week's supply of food and water and its body heat would keep the electrical circuitry warm enough to do its job, i.e. to set off a nuclear explosion killing both thousands of Russians, and the chicken. And Hugh Fearnley-Whittingstall, who was inside worrying about the chicken's living conditions.

Several dozen 'suicide chickens' were recruited for this mission. They were not told their eventual fate. Instead, they were told that the large metal canister into which they were being deposited was a new, experimental type of hen house. This caution was unnecessary, since, as Hugh F-W found out, being buried alive inside a nuclear bomb is preferable to living on a battery farm and, ultimately, the end is quicker and less stressful.

Sadly, however, the gallant British chickens never got the chance to go into action against the Soviets. Project Blue Peacock was cancelled because the people charged with building the device couldn't read the plans without giggling. Papers declassified in 2003 reveal that Anthony Eden wrote a memo in 1955 asking 'Re project Blue Peacock – are they having a laugh, or what?'

They weren't. Google Blue Peacock and check for yourself.

MOST INCOMPREHENSIBLE SCIENTIFIC THEORY

Relativity Relativity says that the speed of light is constant in a vacuum. It is not a very useful theory, since it's quite hard to get light into a vacuum – it's much better to use a Dyson, which is see-through. The theory also claims that as you approach the speed of light you get shorter and shorter, which means that Jon Holmes may be moving at close to 186,000 miles a second.

Quantum mechanics This is so weird that it's said that if you think you've understood it, you haven't read it properly. Only very high-powered physicists understand it, or claim they do. Since I'm not one of them, I'll stop there.

String theory is mental. No, really. Just don't even try.

Chaos theory involves non-linearity – the idea that small changes in input to a system produce large and unpredictable changes in output. This is traditionally expressed by a metaphor which says that 'a butterfly flaps its wings over Tokyo and causes a hurricane in Florida'.

Some American tourists have failed to understand that this is purely metaphorical, and residents in the Japanese capital have observed a strange sight – US visitors chasing butterflies through their streets with cans of Raid, shouting, 'Blow ma cousin's house down, did ya? Take that, ya varmint!'

These records may well be broken by the LARGE HADRON COLLIDER (see *LARGEST MEDIA COVERAGE FOR A PARTICLE-PHYSICS EXPERIMENT*). Truth is, modern science is really hard, and many people prefer to ignore it for this reason. In the United States there is now a movement called 'Common-sense science', which essentially argues that the whole of 20th-century physics was just made up. We don't actually know anything about atoms or how they behave, and quantum mechanics and relativity are just wild guesswork. Quite how this wild guesswork was able to persuade a small lump of metal to explode with enough force to wipe out Hiroshima, 'Common-sense science' doesn't explain.

COOLEST SPACESHIP
OF ALL TIME

Straight choice of three:

USS ENTERPRISE The original *Enterprise* achieved a remarkable reverse-Tardis effect: it was much bigger on the outside than it was on the inside. The exterior showed a vast interstellar vessel. Inside, the flight deck was a small circular room with a wall-mounted TV, and the two huge engines were controlled from a tiny cubby-hole in which Mr Scott would be on the phone to the bridge, shouting about dilithium crystals.

MILLENNIUM FALCON Han Solo's ride. Not only could it make the jump to lightspeed (without worrying that it would, therefore, now have infinite mass), but it could do it with a Wookie as co-pilot. Breaking Einstein's law of relativity is one thing, but breaking it with the help of a big hairy Bigfoot who can't even talk is quite an achievement.

THE ONE IN *INDEPENDENCE DAY* PILOTED BY WILL SMITH AND JEFF GOLDBLUM How brilliantly rubbish is *Independence Day*? This is an alien spaceship designed by things with tentacles – and yet it has controls easily mastered by a mammal with opposable thumbs. It also has computer software which is readily compatible with that of Earth, which is an unlikely coincidence. If we are ever invaded by beings from another galaxy millions of light years away, it is doubtful that we will find they are running Microsoft-compatible software. If they are, it proves that Bill Gates is secretly an alien, as David Icke said all along.

The ending of *Independence Day* – although punch-the-air marvellous – is also one of the officially Most Ridiculous Movie Endings of All Time (see *MOST RIDICULOUS MOVIE ENDINGS OF ALL TIME*). Will Smith and Jeff Goldblum destroy the entire invasion fleet of an advanced alien race by writing a virus on a laptop, and then uploading it into the mothership, thereby blowing it up. The last words heard from the aliens are one of their IT engineers going, 'We did remember to enable the firewall, right?'

MOST POINTLESS iPHONE APPLICATIONS

Apple's iPhone, a phone made cool by putting the letter 'i' in front of it, has doubtless been a runaway success. But then, so was Ronnie Biggs for a long time, running away successfully to South America as he did. What let Mr Biggs down in the end, however, was the fact that he couldn't play MP3s or allow users to surf the internet or download any one of thousands of applications or 'apps' to his screen, ranging from currency converters to a pretend pint of beer.

The market for these applications is huge and these clever bits of software can do anything from turning your phone into a spirit level and making it sound like a lightsabre all the way up to a device that measures exactly how much of an arse you look while wielding the said spirit-levelling lightsabre phone in public. The following are *genuine* applications for the iPhone and jointly hold the record for most pointless:

BABY SHAKER The phone makes a noise like a baby crying. You shake it as hard as you can to make it stop. There's a photo of a baby on the screen. Seriously. When it stops crying, red crosses appear over the baby's eyes. Apple have withdrawn this one for some reason.

IFART The phone makes a noise like a fart. A variety of farts in fact, ranging from 'dry and throaty' to 'wet gasper'. iFart. It's a fart made cool by putting the letter 'i' in front of it. Popular with schoolboys and braying men who work in the City.

TAKE ME TO MY CAR You get out of your car and activate the app. It pinpoints your location via GPS and then, later, guides you back to your car. If you are the sort of person who can't find your way back to your own car, then frankly you and this (cr)app deserve each other.

HOLD IT A big button appears on the phone's screen. You see how long you can hold it. That's it.

POOP THE WORLD Tracks people going for a poo worldwide and pinpoints their location on Google maps. You sign up and then when you do a poo, you simply tell your phone and it tells the world where it is and, optionally, what you think it smells like. Do you think this is what Tim Berners-Lee had in mind when he invented the internet? No, me neither. Still, it's a nice alternative to reading the back of the shampoo bottle for the 200th time.

CRAZY MOUTH Hold your phone sideways in front of your real mouth. Launch the app. On the screen there is a crazy mouth. In front of your real mouth. On a screen. A crazy mouth.

It's a mouth. A crazy mouth. In front of your real mouth. On a screen. This costs £1.19. Or kill yourself. It's better value.

GOOD IDEA Find someone who's bothered to download Hold It and Crazy Mouth or any number of equally mind-draining iPhone applications. Next, take their iPhone forcibly from them, and shove it up their arse.

BEST ENGINEER

There's only one famous engineer – ISAMBARD KINGDOM BRUNEL. Everyone's heard of him. He built bridges, boats and the Great Western Railway. Everyone likes Brunel, to the extent that if there's a delay on the line into Paddington, they will make an announcement saying, 'There are signaling problems in the Reading area, but it's nothing to do with Brunel. All his bits are fine. Bridges, tunnels – all working. It's us. We're crap.'

BEST ENGINEERING NATION

By common consent, GERMANY is the best engineering country. German cars, dishwashers and cookers are generally considered the most reliable in the world. This reputation came about largely in the 1970s and 1980s, owing largely to comparisons between the Volkswagen, Audi and BMW and British Leyland. (It was the choice between the Austin Princess and the Volkswagen

Golf that finally, after 35 years, persuaded the British to forget about the war.)

The most obvious proof of the superiority of German engineering is seen in the fact that several times a year, an unexploded Second World War bomb is found in a British city and the whole area has to be evacuated. The Army have to be called in and the device made safe because even though it's been buried in the ground for nearly seventy years, it's *still dangerous and might go off*. That's the build quality of German engineering. By contrast, in 2006 a British bomb was found unexploded in Köln; the Germans threw it into a skip, shouting, 'Don't worry The fuses were from Curry's and the extended warranty ran out in 1947.'

MOST UNCONVINCING-SOUNDING INGREDIENT IN A SKINCARE PRODUCT

The most unconvincing sounding ingredient in a skincare product is Boswellox, one of a range of beauty ingredients developed by notable biographers and diarists. (Pepysox, Ackroydox and Lady Antonia Fraserox are expected by the end of the year.)

In the adverts, Boswelox is spelt with one 'l', because a certain well-known brand has probably copyrighted it – but it should have two. They've taken it from Boswellia (with both 'll's), which is the botanical name for a whole load of plants whose resin is a traditional ingredient in herbal medicine. One of the plants, *Boswellia sacra*, is the source of frankincense, the biblical gift given by the Three Wise Men to the baby Jesus. Why they would give a newborn baby a wrinkle-removal product is unclear. It seems more likely that the gold and myrrh were for Jesus, while the Boswellia product was intended for Mary. In some apocryphal fragments, Mary thanks the Wise Men for their gifts and asks what she has done to deserve them – to which Melchior replies 'because you're worth it'.

MOST INFURIATING TIME FOR MICROSOFT WORD TO CRASH

This is commonly thought to be in the early hours of the morning during the final paragraph of an essay due to be handed in by a student at 9 a.m. While this is true for those in higher education, once the world of work is brought into the equation, the infuriating nature of MS Word crashes becomes much more pronounced. The most infuriating time on record for MS Word to crash suddenly in a work-related environment happened in 2003 to Michael Zanowski, chief speech writer to then President of the United States of America, George W. Bush. Just as Mr Zanowski was putting the finishing touches to an eloquent speech about education, MS Word experienced what it called 'an illegal operation' and was shut down. There were just minutes to go before President Bush had to deliver the speech but when Word was rebooted there was only one font available, so Mr Zanowski was quickly forced to write the remainder of the President's speech in Wingdings (see *FONT, MOST POINTLESS*). Even though it now made no sense and was just a confusing jumble of shapes and half-words, it was handed to Bush who simply read it verbatim. During Mr Bush's tenure in the White House, word processing software crashes of this nature happened on many occasions, which would explain a lot.

MOST POINTLESS FEATURE ON A TELEVISION

Without doubt, the most pointless feature on a television, or indeed any electrical appliance, is 'stand-by'.

Why would you keep your television on stand-by? When are you going to need your telly at that level of readiness? Stand-by is for fighter squadrons or firemen, not telly watching. Watching telly really isn't that important. No self respecting Pathe Newsreel ever went:

> 'All across Britain squadrons of televisions are kept at the highest level of preparedness so that they can instantly cope with any emergency that may come their way. They wait patiently for the tannoy, the tannoy which will tell them to scramble, to scramble as fast as they are able, or they might miss the beginning of Hollyoaks.'

FOOD
AND
DRINK

WORLD'S MOST OVER-ELABORATE COFFEE

The Double-Whip Mocha-Choc Cinnamon Tall Skinny Frappuccino held sway in this category until the introduction of the Medio-Grande Doppio Cappadappadabbadoo Soyspresso With Sprinkles, but this is so revolting that no one has ever finished one. So it doesn't count.

SWEARIEST CHEF

The first rule of Cookery Club is the posher the food, the more the chef swears. The people on the griddle in McDonald's never seem to shout very much except to confirm things are ready. The people dropping star anise into a lobster nage in some Michelin-starred *poncerie*, on the other hand, bellow at each other like drunken sailors on a night out. This makes for a very strange atmosphere. Fast food is accompanied by shouts of 'quarter-pounders ready'. Posh food is accompanied by shouts of 'call that a f******asparagus foam, you ****?'

For many years the swearing was all in French, so no one cared or minded. More recently, however, it has become *de rigeur* for a top chef to be a swearmeister in their native tongue. Most foul-mouthed drunks with a knife would be arrested; but if they're in a posh kitchen making a flambé, an exception is made.

The sweariest chef of all is, of course, GORDON RAMSAY, but don't be fooled. It's all part of his branding. Interviewed on the radio promoting his autobiography, he was asked whether all the cussing was strictly necessary. Ramsey explained that it was all due to his passion; that the atmosphere in a kitchen is high pressured and fraught; that he cares so much about his work that he effs and blinds in the heat of the moment. There was a perfect pause before Simon Mayo said, 'But, Gordon – it's all the way through your book.'

WORST-TASTING PETROL GARAGE FORECOURT SHOP PASTY OR SNACK

Your average petrol station forecourt shop is full of foul snacks, and anyone on a long journey who's ever been forced to eat one because there's nothing else left will have difficulty deciding which one is the worst or least appetising. Some say it's a beef 'slice', while others argue for the intrinsic unpleasantness of a Scotch Egg, but in fact it's neither of these. Granted, anything from the the well-known 'slice' range will leave the inside of your mouth feeling dry and pasty, like it's been jetwashed with eczema, but the very worst food item by quite some distance is that thing that's a sort of crumb-coated oblong meat tube rammed full of coleslaw and cheese. A Buffet Bar, they call it. It's an effrontery to the oral cavity; to eat one is like being waterboarded with stodgy filling. Yes, that's it. The Buffet Bar. That's definitely the worst. Although Hugh Dennis really likes them.

MOST BUFFET LEFT OVER AFTER A WEDDING

This was the wedding reception of David Billingsley and Emma Whitehead at Sittingbourne Working Men's Club, in Kent on 14 August 2010. The couple had invited 100 guests for the day and a further 30 in the evening and had foolishly catered for them all. At the end, scientists measured an enormous surplus of dry corned-beef sandwiches, vol-au-vents with an unidentifiable filling, damp quiche and small round things in breadcrumbs that could have been either chicken or fish or cheese. No crisps were left, despite some of them being horrible prawn cocktail Skips (See *CRISPS, MOST UNPLEASANT FLAVOUR*). At the end of the night when the disco had finished, all remaining food was binned by the club, prompting one of the bar staff (female) to tut and say 'what a waste' as she helped herself to one of the remaining samosas.

PONCIEST CELEB-CHEF MUCKED-ABOUT DISH

Celebrity chefs cannot just tell you how to make a classic dish. Inevitably they will insist on giving you 'my take on this classic dish' − the phrase 'my take' being a big, flashing warning sign. It always means, 'Here is a classic dish which I've pissed about with, pointlessly and needlessly, in order to justify the advance for my book.'

Let's say you want to know how to make beans on toast.

You turn to your recipe book by Jamie Ramseystein-Whittingella, and it will say something like:

> 'Here is my take on the classic beans on toast. Instead of shop-bought beans, I've used home-grown organic haricots from my own garden, cooked in an authentic Breton marmite with a deseeded Tuscan tomato reduction. If you can't get home-grown beans, you can use a tin of Heinz, but you're a pleb. For the toast, I like to use a slice of home-baked rosemary-infused sourdough, but you can use Mother's Pride, although you are a feckless chav if you do. In fact, why have you bought a cookery book at all? You're basically scum.'

The only exception to this rule is Delia, who wrote a book called *Lazy Arse Cooking for Stingy Bastards*, or something. Can't remember the actual title, but she got pilloried for it.

MOST VISITS TO SALAD CART

For those who frequent certain types of restaurant – usually large family-friendly ones with faux farming implements on the walls and chicken wings on the menu – a 'visit to the salad cart' will be a familiar ritual. Usually found lurking in Harvester- or Beefeater-style establishments and oft prefixed by the word 'unlimited', a visit to the salad cart will frequently be chosen in lieu of a proper starter by the sort of people who 'want to get their money's worth'.

At first glance, the salad cart may, of course, appear to be the healthy option; a dietary alternative to the likes of 'loaded skins' or 'breaded mushrooms' that clog up both the menu and your arteries in one fell swoop of deep-fried calories in batter. The fact is that the food on a salad cart could only really be described as salad in the loosest possible sense. Creamy cold pasta with bits of sausage in it is not salad. It's creamy cold sausage pasta, is what it is, and is certainly not recommended, as salad is, as one of your five a day. Not unless your five a day are five plates of creamy cold sausage pasta, a health option surely frowned upon by all but the most lazy and haphazard nutritionist. Mayonnaise-drenched lumps of gangrenous potato do also not constitute salad. Neither do rollmop herrings to my mind, nor eight boiled eggs, nor more pasta, nor so-called 'bacon bits' which purport to be bits of bacon but are in fact just dusty bits of synthetic inedible grit.

The other problem is that word 'unlimited'. One may have chosen the help oneself to the salad option with all the good intentions in the world, but the temptation to 'get one's money's worth' by piling up one's plate, covering it all in both blue cheese *and* thousand island dressing and then going back for a second lot before the main course arrives is overwhelming. Of course there *is* salad at a salad bar (lettuce, cucumber, tomatoes and so forth), but ironically for said bar it tends to get largely passed over and ignored in favour of the stuff that's decidedly un-saladlike, making it the green-leaf equivalent of the plain girl at a school disco who sat in the corner and failed to get off with anyone because she was boring. Furthermore, because it's the salad cart (or salad 'bar' as more upmarket crap restaurants insist on calling it), psychologically speaking, your brain thinks, 'Aha – I can eat loads of this, it's delicious healthy salad. If it's on the salad cart it must be of the genus ìsaladî,' and thus sends signals to your fat face, telling it to stuff as many rollmops down its porky throat as it can before the waitress notices that you've been back and forth to the evil cart more times than a medieval plague undertaker collecting the dead.

The world record for most visits to a salad cart in one sitting goes to me and my friend Andy Hurst who once, on a ferry trip from Portsmouth to Spain, availed ourselves of the salad cart in the onboard restaurant so much that, by the time the main course arrived, we could barely speak or lift cutlery. We counted 14 trips between us to the salad cart, continually returning to its healthy unlimited goodness like greedy moths to a flambéed prawn skewer. Even though we were so stuffed full of rollmop that our stomachs meant that the *Pride of Bilbao* had now sunk lower in the water and everyone was in danger, still we returned, crawling sluggishly back towards the coleslaw. That night, we were determined to beat the salad cart but, alas, it claimed us, round about the point of the crabsticks, and we were forced to concede defeat. The next morning, when asked by our then girlfriends what the hell we thought we'd been doing, we invoked the spirit of Sir Edmund Hillary: 'Why the holy hell were you two stuffing yourselves with pasta and bacon bits when your main course was arriving in a moment? Why did you keep going back to the salad cart and then coming back to the table with anything *but* salad? Why were you trying to beat the salad cart?'

We looked them in the eye from where we were unable to get out of our bunks, and our answer was as simple as our meal had not been.

Because it was there. JH

THE MOST EXPENSIVE BISCUIT IN HISTORY

Is the Duchy Original Oaten biscuit costing as much as £10,000 per bite. Fortunately the biscuits are subsidised by Prince Charles, halving their actual cost to just £37,000 per box. Organic deliciousness. MB

MOST BAFFLING FOOD LABEL

Many products come with information designed to reassure the consumer that they are buying something ethically sourced. Animal products especially come with a great deal of lifestyle information about the living conditions of the now-deceased creatures that are heading for your dinner table.

I once bought some chicken from a leading supermarket which was not quite free-range, so they couldn't call it that, so instead, the label said, 'From birds allowed to roam on open ground in hours of daylight.' This phrasing was not reassuring at all. I was clearly meant to think, 'Oh good, it's been allowed to run about a bit and not stuck in a shed,' but actually, what I found myself thinking was, 'I don't want to eat chicken that can't be trusted after dark,' Why was this chicken under curfew? Further along in the same meat compartment was pork 'From pigs grounded under the terms of their ASBO', and some more expensive chicken 'From birds allowed out at night on condition they take a taxi home'.

This type of label could, of course, have provided the Countryside Alliance with a useful tool to attack the foxhunting ban. Chicken could be sold in packaging that says, 'From birds kept in at night so they don't get savaged by the foxes you metropolitan bloody liberals are so keen to save.'

This kind of labelling is only used, you notice, when there is positive information to give. You never buy vegetables that say 'Harvested by under-paid immigrants for a pittance' or fish-fingers that proudly tell you that they are 'From an unsustainable source, trawled by a Russian factory-ship in contravention of international quotas',

MADDEST CHEF

Britain's maddest chef is, of course, HESTON BLUMENTHAL, aka Berkshire's Willy Wonka. Heston realised early doors that all possible angles on the celebrity chef had been covered, except for one.

ANGLE	POSITION FILLED BY
Enthusiastic mockney yoof	**Jamie**
Grumpy old fish-botherer	**Rick**
Mumsy and dependable	**Delia**
Mumsy and foxy as hell	**Nigella**
Sweary genius	**Gordon Ramsay** (see *CHEF, SWEARIEST*)
Posh eccentric	**Hugh Fearnley-Whittingstall**
Housewives' choice	**Ainsley Harriott**
Dirty housewives' choice	**James Martin**
Comedy drunk	**Keith Floyd**

Heston immediately realised there was a gap in the market for mad scientist liquid-hydrogen-wielding nutter, and went for it big time. He's great. We love Heston.

Blumenthal is famous for using rigorous scientific methods and his knowledge of the chemical constituents in never-thought-of-before combinations of taste and texture. Brilliant, although all he has really done is write down the culinary concoctions of drunk people scavenging in the fridge and kitchen after a hard night out. If you don't believe me compare the following:

Concoctions of Drunk People

- *Alpen with Vodka and a side dish of Toast with Ketchup*
- *A Pork Pie with Marmalade, Skimmed Milk and some cold Beans*
- *Half an Onion from the composter, Müller Yoghurt, Lettuce and a Cream Cracker*

Concoctions from The Fat Duck Tasting Menu

- *Snail porridge*
- *Parsnip Cereal*
- *Nitro Scrambled Egg and Bacon Ice Cream*
- *Apple Pie Caramel in Edible Wrapper*
- *Pommery Grain Mustard Ice Cream Red Cabbage Gazpacho*

The only difference is that Heston has thoughtfully made the caramel wrapper edible, because he knows that when you're a bit gone you are going to eat it anyway.

Heston and his fellow British chefs have presided over

a revolution in the United Kingdom's cuisine, although there still seems to be a rule that the French are best at cookery. Why? Because they are in charge of the Michelin Star system and we accept it. Michelin make tyres for goodness sake – how can they be arbiters of good food? They can't. Except, possibly, for fans of Old Jokes Involving Comedy Chinese Pronunciation – hence the phrase 'this chicken is rubbery'.

(See *OLDEST JOKE INVOLVING COMEDY CHINESE PRONUNICIATION*.)

MOST BORINGEST CHOCOLATE

Crunchie? Milky Bar? Blue Riband? There really is some dull confectionery on offer, isn't there? And be honest, who among us hasn't died a little bit inside when, upon eating a bag of Revels, you keep getting a Malteser? Maltesers should not be hiding in Revels. Maltesers have got their own corner of the market, dominated solely by Maltesers, so please stop hiding them in a bag of otherwise pleasant chocolates like some kind of dreary, honeycomb-centred cuckoo in the nest. Thus, MALTESERS are the World's Boringest Chocolate.

Milky Bars are dull, too. One bite – interesting. A curious chocolate experience. I see what you've done there. It's a different colour, you're experimenting with the form. Next bite – mm . . . bit sickly and slightly odd tasting but still, it's a bit different. Third bite – meh. Yuck. In the bin.

Blue Ribands are also tedious because there is quite simply far too much wafer. Just as the surface of the earth is mostly water and the inside of the human body is mostly water, the taste of a Blue Riband is mostly wafer. The chocolate-to-wafer ratio is all wrong. Given one taste of a Blue Riband, Willy Wonka, if he were real and dead, would be turning in his grave. And while we're on the subject, why hasn't someone invented all the excellent sweets that Roald Dahl dreamt up? Everlasting Gobstoppers? Lickable Wallpaper? Three Course Dinner Chewing Gum? Come on Cadbury's, pull your finger out. The most interesting thing you've got is a Boost. And don't get me started on Crunchies. BORING. It's just like eating a long, rectangular Malteser, and we all know how lacklustre they are.

NB The runner-up for the title of Most Boringest Chocolate goes to the band Hot Chocolate for their song 'Everyone's a Winner'. No, they are not. Everyone is not a winner. Certainly not whoever came up with the idea for Maltesers anyway.

BEST SIDE EFFECT OF CREDIT CRUNCH

The credit crunch has had a positive side, which is to put an end to the ever-increasing profusion of pointless 'luxury' products in fields where 'luxury' products have no place at all – notably in the field of snacks. And, specifically, crisps.

Once upon a time, crisps were just crisps. They came in small plastic bags in a range of flavours and had no pretensions at all. They were just crisps, and their varieties were suitably proletarian – salt'n'vinegar with its fish-and-chip-shop overtones, Bovril with its connotations of football terraces, and cheese and onion, with its vague feeling of ploughman's lunch in a bag.

But an opportunity was spotted by the marketing wonks.

Profits could be bigger if the public could be convinced that crisps were a 'luxury' product rather than something you got out of a machine after swimming. Crisps had the potential to move upmarket.

The snack counter then became the British class system in retail form. At one end, small cheap bags made of crinkly see-through polythene, containing things like Frazzles and Monster Munch and Hula Hoops. At the other end, vast pillow-sized bags in muted colours saying things like 'Hand-Cut Pan-Fried Sea-Salt and Balsamic Vinegar New England Potato Chips'. What these are, are crisps. But they cost about three quid a bag and are designed to convince the middle-class Waitrose-going consumer that they are not eating some unhealthy snack like the chavs do. No. These are a sophisticated and nutritious addition to their lifestyle, designed to be eaten in exalted company and accompanying the finest wines. There's only one problem with this theory – *they're crisps*. If it looks like a crisp, tastes like a crisp and sounds like a crisp, it's a crisp, even if it's duck à l'orange flavour and contained in a waxed hand-sealed bag.

The packaging of these sorts of things ought to be set for GCSE English. You could spend hours analysing the sheer stupidity of the jargon used to sell these jumped-up slices of fried potato. There are now crisps which tell you *what breed of potato* they're made from. (The principle of Nazi snack policy, incidentally. Hitler refused to eat 'mongrel tubers'.)

There are crisps that stress the fact that *the skin is left on*. Which is important, because – after being submerged twice in boiling oil – that's where the vitamins used to be. There are crisps that stress that they're *'fried in pressed sunflower oil'* or *'lightly dusted with flakes of naturally dried Guérande sea salt'* or *'individually cut by a Michelin-starred chef with a silver knife hand-sharpened by a trained Gurkha'* or *'made from potatoes individually traceable back to the original sackful brought home by Sir Walter Raleigh in 1589'* – none of which alters the fact that they are, in the end, just crisps. The financial crisis has made a big dent in the sales of these absurd products, which is excellent. If you want to pretend that potato crisps are posh, then why not do it in the time-honoured British way, and buy them a peerage?

FOOD-HYGIENE INNOVATION MOST IGNORED BY OLDER PEOPLE

The older generation simply have no time for SELL-BY or EAT-BY DATES, and rely instead on a combination of smelling, poking, feeling and scraping food they think might be off, and the sturdiness of their own battle-hardened digestive systems to see them through safely. And you can see their point – food beyond the eat-by date isn't necessarily unsafe, and in these recessionary times you don't voluntarily want to lob uneaten food in the bin, or bulge the profits of the supermarkets by buying more as soon as the magic date arrives.

What we really need is a series of dates which better reflect the way we live our lives. By all means keep a 'best before date', but in addition include the following:

An 'Oh, for heaven's sake, it'll be fine' date

A '100 years ago people ate stuff that colour all the time' date

A 'Just scrape the mould off the top, it's fine at the bottom' date

.... ◈ ....

And finally:

An 'Actually this does smell a bit off, but I've just had six pints of lager and I am really, really hungry' date

The last, of course, would be best used on food aimed at students.

MOST MALIGNED FOODSTUFFS

There are various foods which are, inexplicably, the subject of constant ridicule, contempt and loathing. The current leaders are:

BRUSSELS SPROUTS Every Christmas there are dozens and dozens of jokes, insults and abuse directed at these humble mini-cabbages. Most of them are about how farty they are, and this is true – they are. However, it is also frequently implied that they don't taste nice and have a horrible texture. Neither of these things is true. If the British didn't overcook everything by boiling it to death like we were still living in the 1950s, then it would be perfectly obvious that sprouts are really quite nice. (But farty.)

FISH People who don't like fish are really annoying. As far back as the 1930s, marketing experts knew very well that when people claim they don't like something, it's often to cover up the fact that they've *never been brave enough to try it*. Many people who whinge about fish have never eaten anything other than a fish finger or a McDonald's Filet. It's actually pretty much impossible to eat smoked haddock, or a piece of grilled halibut, without discovering that this stuff tastes *really very nice indeed*. The strange thing is that although lots of people claim they don't like fish, we are somehow managing to wipe out most of the edible species. It can't all be the Japanese, surely. Maybe the people that like fish keep it secret. The last thing they want is the chavs stuffing down the few remaining cod.

PORRIDGE People are too lazy to make porridge. So they claim they don't like it. The only people to regularly ingest this magnificent slop are the Scots – they have time to make it, because in winter in Scotland it doesn't get light until lunchtime.

MOST UNPLEASANT CRISP FLAVOUR

At the other, or 'arse', end of the crisp market it has become fashionable for purveyors of crisp-based snacks to add a variety of unlikely flavours to their maize-based oeuvre. These add a 'taste sensation' to hitherto crisp standards such as Cheese'n'Onion or Beef. Unusual flavours have included *Cajun Squirrel*, *Chilli & Chocolate*, *Builder's Breakfast* and the hastily withdrawn *Gents Public Toilet Floor*. But these are by no means the most unpleasant crisp flavours available. Some are listed below:

- Yellow Snow
- Germoline 'n' Onion
- Poo Sticks
- Flobby Bovril

- Cheesy Nik Nackers
- First Time Bungee Jumper's Pants
- Golden Wonder Salty MILFs
- Crispy Pork Swords
- Nappy Rash Frazzles
- Glade Plug-In 'n' Chive Pringles
- Prawn Cock

Unpleasant though these may sound and/or taste, they pale into insignificance when put up against the most revolting crisp ever made in terms of texture and taste. This, and the record holder by miles, is a single packet of KP prawn cocktail Skips.

BIGGEST SHOCK
TO SOUTHERNERS

Peter Kay's famous 'garlic bread' routine was all based on the notion that his father found the concept of garlic bread laughable and strange – *in the late 1990s*. Southerners had stopped finding garlic funny by the early 1980s, and were totally baffled by the idea that there were northerners – even older ones – who still thought it was foreign food. They sat watching their Peter Kay DVDs in bemused silence, thinking, 'But my dad loves garlic bread. In fact, he sometimes makes it himself.'

It was a huge shock to southerners, and also a bit of a relief. After the Britpop years and the success of Oasis and Robbie Williams, many of them were secretly starting to wonder whether northerners were cooler and hipper than them. After Peter Kay did 'garlic bread', southerners relaxed, knowing that northerners were still just how they imagined.

MOST POPULAR
HOT BEVERAGE

The most popular hot beverage in the world is COFFEE, with approximately 7 million metric tonnes being produced and consumed every year.

Since first being brewed in 9th-century Ethiopia, coffee has been much prized for its restorative and stimulatory properties. It has become a staple resource of police officers, night-shift workers and comic songwriters who've agreed to contribute to a radio show spin-off book despite it being a book and, therefore, having no songs in, but now realise the due date is tomorrow and they'd better write something, so were thrashing around for a subject when . . . ah! Coffee! Popular blends include French Roast, Brazilian, Italian Espresso and Benn's Patent Deadline Buster, a particularly lethal concoction consisting of five spoonfuls of Tesco's economy freeze-dried, nine sugars and Coffee Mate. While the drink's usefulness as a stimulant and general pick-me-up (nice phrase, why doesn't anyone use it any more?) is undoubted, doctors warn that excessive consumption of caffeine can lead to palpitations, cardiac arrhythmia, the shakes, and lossss off cooooordddinaataionaoaanannnn . . . n . . .

(phhhhhhhhh . . .)

Okay. We're okay. FFWWWuh huh.

Further research suggests that overuse of coffee, combined

with the resultant sleeplessness, can lead to paranoia, delusions and panic attacks, but that's just what they *would* say, isn't it? Bastards. What are they after? I see them, they're everywhere, they follow me about, you know, they think I can't see them but I see *them*, ha ha ha, I'm onto you, you invisible little – *Waagh! What's that? What is it?! It's coming! It's coming to get me! Help! Heeeelp!*

Doctors say that someone in this condition can generally be snapped out of it with a good hard slap. (Thanks, darling. Ow!)

Once caffeine has passed through the system, withdrawal symptoms can include headaches, nausea and a feeling of guilt (I'm so sorry, baby, could you please get me a couple of Nurofen). The stimulating effect will wear off quite rapidly – yaawwn – and be replaced with crippling fatigue, which soon resultsss innnzzzzzzzzzzzzzzzzzzzzzzzzzzzzzz . . .

(See *COFFEE, WORLD'S MOST OVER ELABORATE*.) MB

WEIRDEST CONSUMER SURVEY

The current holder in this category is the following survey, published in September 2005:

> 'The age-old myth that cheese gives you nightmares has finally been laid to rest this week following the release of a new study carried out by the British Cheese Board. The in-depth Cheese & Dreams study, a first of its kind, reveals that eating cheese before bed will not only aid

.... ☕ ....

> a good night's sleep but different cheeses will in fact
> cause different types of dreams.'

That's right – *different cheeses will cause different types of dreams.*
Some actual researchers *actually researched this and were actually
paid to do it.*

Why on earth would anyone bother? Well, the first thing to do
with this kind of survey is look at who commissioned it. In this
case, it was the British Cheese Board. They asked 200 volunteers
to 'eat a 20g piece of cheese half an hour before going to sleep'
and then recorded the results. The results, amazingly, showed
that, guess what? Cheese doesn't give you nightmares at all.
Quite the opposite. If the results are to be believed, cheese is
a recreational drug like no other, providing uppers, downers,
hallucinogens and sedatives, all perfectly legal. If you want to
trip out on cheese, the survey found that:

> 'Over 65% of participants eating Red Leicester revisited
> their schooldays.'

So, if you fancy waking up thinking about your old geography
teacher, Red Leicester's the stuff for you. Then there's the king
of British cheese, Stilton, apparently gives you the dairy
equivalent of an acid trip.

> '85% of females who ate Stilton had some of the most
> unusual dreams of the whole study.'

Plasticine porters with looking-glass ties. I looked in the sky at
an elephant's eye. Man, this stuff is groovy. Or maybe it's the
port? Sadly, it doesn't work for men. Males will have to go for
Lancashire.

'Two-thirds of all those who ate Lancashire had a dream about work.'

This is not what writers and artists are supposed to dream about. When Samuel Taylor Coleridge woke from his opium trance to write his masterpiece, it didn't start 'In Xanadu did Kubla Khan, some urgent e-mails and did a bit of photocopying'. So, what about plain old-fashioned Cheddar?

'65% of people eating Cheddar dreamt about celebrities.'

So there you are. If you want to dream of a chav knees-up with some minor soapstars, an *X-Factor* judge or a footballer's girlfriend, fire up the grill and get the bread out. You can take your cheddar raw, or mix it with Stilton, toast it and snort the fumes.

This survey is still the weirdest, although subsequent research has shown that there are holes in the theory. And, indeed in the cheese. The major objection is that if the cheesy dreams theory is correct, you really need to carry out a survey in France. If the British are experiencing noticeable after-dinner effects, then the French must sleep in a psychedelic stupor. Which might explain a lot, including cubism, bouncy cars and their inability to understand traffic lights.

RESTAURANT FOOD THAT, WHEN IT FINALLY ARRIVES, LOOKS LEAST LIKE ITS PICTURE ON THE MENU

Look at that plump burger. All succulent and juicy and sitting on a crisp bed of lettuce, droplets of fresh water still visible on its sparkling green leaves, the tomato, like lipstick left on your cheek from your first kiss, ripe, bursting with flavour. And the bun sandwiching the sizzling meat like a fluffy moon of bread, the top dusted with sesame seeds, promising a lightness beyond measure. So why, when it arrives, does your hamburger look like it's been squashed in a tramp's pocket for a few days and is limper than George Osbourne's handshake?

As a teenager, Jon once frequented 'restaurants' called Julie's Pantry and ordered something called a *COUNTRYBURGER* which, according to the description and accompanying photograph, was 'a succulent quarter-pounder of 100% sizzling American beef cooked to perfection and served on a bed of crisp iceberg lettuce with slices of plump tomato on a toasted sesame seed bun dressed up with American Cheese and home-made mayo for that pure fresh country taste!' (The exclamation mark was theirs.)

What arrived, was a flaccid mulch of beige with a tepid half-pink thing in it that had both the texture and thinness of a mouse-mat with Aids. There was something green lurking in there but on closer inspection it was in fact less 'crisp iceberg lettuce' and more 'layer of thin gruel', while the bun was like two halves of the wet, floppy gloop that wouldn't be out of place filling those small bags you see being inserted into ladies' chests on various Channel 5 bodyshock documentaries.

Julie's Pantry is no more, probably because Julie finally realised the futility of it all and ended it by deep-frying herself in her own onion ring machine. Next morning at 5 a.m., her blistered, battered and charred corpse was fished out by bleary-eyed staff in bonnets and served to the day's first customer as 'a delicious, crispy, full-flavoured, hot 'n' spicy, crunchy-coated treat with a choice of dip'. JH

HUMAN
ACHIEVEMENT

WORLD'S STRONGEST MAN

The winner of this category is whoever wins that weird TV show which nowadays is on Five. The depressing thing about *World's Strongest Man* is that Spider-Man was wrong – with great power doesn't come great responsibility, but enormous pointlessness. Rather than use their powers for good, the world's strongest men have to pull trucks with a harness (join the AA, for God's sake), put rocks on stands (useful for landscape gardeners) and generally perform circus tricks. If they're really the world's strongest men, they ought to be able to get their agent in a headlock and say 'get me something more useful to do'.

MOST OBVIOUS MANIFESTATION OF MIDDLE-CLASS STATUS

Middle-class parents are almost paranoically unimaginative when it comes to naming their offspring. They like to call their sons Jack, Tom or Harry, like they're escape tunnels rather than children. Girls are given names like Victorian dolls – Emily, Chloe or Bronchitis.

The working class, on the other hand, give free rein to their imaginations, naming their children after rappers, foreign surnames, sports stars, holiday destinations or anything that takes their fancy. Frequently these names are then misspelt. (Britney Spears almost had a brother called Dordoyn. This was deemed to be a bit too upmarket, so in the end he was christened Coat Dazzur.)

POSHEST
SURNAME

If the poshest surname in Britain is that of the poshest family in Britain, then pride of place goes to the name Windsor – but that is ridiculous because it doesn't sound posh at all, and every Frank, Harry and Barbara is called Windsor. Of course, the fact it sounds a bit common is deliberate because Windsor is just a surname made up by George V to distract attention from the fact that his original surname, Saxe-Coburg We're-German-Hande-Hoch-For-You-Tommy-The-War-Is-Over Gotha, was quite likely to confuse the British public when we were fighting an extraordinarily bloody conflict with the forces of the Kaiser. So, as a PR exercise, and to avoid bricks being thrown through each of the 900 windows of Buckingham Palace, he chose the name Windsor from a shortlist of three possibles: Windsor, Network-Rail and Sellafield. He eventually chose Windsor because it was already associated with the Royal Family, so we can count ourselves lucky he didn't go with Simpleton, Gaffe-Prone or Horseface.

As a result of George's tinkering, the poshest surnames in Britain are now the preserve of lower divisions of the aristocracy where the sheer unwillingness of the very posh to let any part of their aristocratic provenance be extinguished from the record has resulted in surnames of quite ludicrous length. Indeed, were it not for the fact that so many upper-class families are ex-directory, the Gloucestershire phone book would need 12 volumes simply to cover the first four names of the letter A.

From this divison of the aristocracy there are many candidates for who has the poshest name, among them, Anstruther Gough Calthorpe, Vane Tempest Stewart and Pugh Pugh Barney McGrew Cuthbert Dibble-Grubb. On the simple basis of the greatest number of hyphens, however, the poshest name in Britain is generally thought to be that of a gentleman called Leone Sextus Denys Oswolf Fraudatifilius Tollemache-Tollemache de Orellana Plantagenet Tollemache-Tollemache, who lived in the early years of the 20th century, and had a son, which is remarkable because in an age of greater formality than our own, he couldn't normally even fully introduce himself to a girl before she fell asleep through boredom.

In any case, the number of hyphens is a very unreliable guide to poshness. Indeed the very poshest are recognisable by the fact that they don't use their hyphens at all, and reduce their names to the briefest possible. If, for example, you are lucky enough to be a Lord you will simply take the name of your title and may therefore be known as Melchett, Buckingham or Scricket-Ground.

In short, this is a ridiculous category and no definitive answer can be given. I wish I hadn't started writing it frankly. HD

BIGGEST MASS-KILLER
IN HISTORY

You're probably thinking Genghis Khan or Vlad the Impaler or Pol Pot or someone, but no. SIR WALTER RALEIGH is the single most life-threatening person in history. He returned to

Europe from the New World in the late 16th century, bringing
with him two things – potatoes and tobacco. *That's fags and
chips.* Smoking and junk food, the two biggest killers of Western
lifestyle – all down to one man in a cloak and a feathery hat.*
He shouldn't have been knighted, he should have been put back
on his boat and told not to return until he'd discovered tofu
and jogging.

** Probably. It might be one of those lazy historical myths that QI are so fond of exposing,
like the one about 'kangaroo' being Aborigine for 'I don't know'. (See BIGGEST
HISTORICAL MYTH WE WON'T GO INTO BECAUSE WE'RE NOT QI.)*

BIGGEST
FALSE ECONOMY

The BBC's budget cuts are not always having the desired effect.
In 2008, guidelines were issued requiring producers to use
the cheapest available taxi company – rather than, say, the
most competent. The effect of this was that when *The Now Show*
recorded in Portsmouth (on the south coast) in June of that
year, the cast was driven back to London by a driver who didn't
know the way. He went off round the M25, refusing all advice
and listening only to his sat-nav, and came into London from the
north-west, reaching Broadcasting House an hour and a half late.
Three further taxis, at after-midnight rates, then had to be booked
to take home the three people who had been expecting to be
dropped off en route. The whole thing, therefore, cost the licence
payer far more than if they'd used a proper cab firm to start
with. The annoying thing is, if we'd been MPs, we could have got
a helicopter instead.

WORLD'S WORST SOOTHSAYER

There are two candidates in this category – Nostradamus and God. The same problem applies to both of them – they are both able to give uncanny predictions of events once the events have happened. Sadly, they never seem to be able to predict them beforehand, or if they do, the predictions are wrong.

God, of course, can't possibly get predictions wrong, as he is omniscient and knows everything that's going to happen. For this reason, he apparently chose to put his predictions into the Bible in the form of very complicated codes which can only be deciphered by non-fiction authors. Sadly, most of them refer to things that have already happened.

This leaves NOSTRADAMUS, who cunningly wrote all his predictions in gibberish that could mean absolutely anything. His most famous quatrain runs:

> **When the hairy house of the bees is seen**
> **The woman shall lean to left and right**
> **Millions of metal eyes surround**
> **But she shall sing at the place of the lost King.**

This is an uncanny premonition of Amy Winehouse's appearance at Glastonbury.

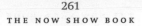

MOST PREDICTABLY IRRITATING SMART-ARSE, KNOW-ALL THING TO SAY WHENEVER ANYONE MENTIONS BIG BEN

'The thing is, Big Ben is actually the name of the bell, not the clock tower.'

MOST EMBARRASSING MOMENT FOR HUGH DENNIS

In 2006 I had to have a colonoscopy, a hideously embarrassing medical procedure in which a camera on a long tube is pushed deep into your lower intestine via the handily placed orifice that is your posterior, so that doctors can have a good long look around, work out what is going on up there, and record it all to DVD. Not entirely aware of the potential pain involved, I decided initially to have this done while still conscious, but my consultant told me I wouldn't thank him 'after the first 2 or 3 feet' so I opted instead to go under general anaesthetic. I was, however, aware of the massive personal embarrassment I would feel if I met anyone I knew at the hospital, so rather than go in London where I had always lived, I opted to go to a very small private hospital near my new home in Sussex. All went well. There was no one I knew in the waiting room. I was greeted by my consultant and his assistant and shown to a room where I was instructed to strip and put on a surgical gown. Now entirely in the care of people who understood discretion and medical confidentiality, I was shown into theatre and asked to lie on a trolley before my gown was pulled back to expose my buttocks to medical staff. I was injected with anaesthetic, and just about to drift into the unconsciousness which would numb the pain of the most humiliating moment of my life when, with a surprisingly wide tube in hand all ready for insertion where the sun don't shine, the nurse turned to me and said:

'I'm a very good friend of your next-door neighbour.' HD

MADDEST ROYAL

History is littered with bonkers heads of state. Most famously, King George III was as mad as a hatter who had drunk way more than his recommended five-a-day portion of mercury, but notable accounts of mental sovereigns go back much further than that. Historians now agree that the very first mad 'royal' was the bearded leader of a Neolithic tribe, and evidence for this was discovered in a cave painting in France by archaeologists in 1940. In one scene in the painting, the tribe leader is seen drinking heavily in a busy cave at night and in the next he is depicted with his arm round some leggy blonde cavegirl as they both stagger out of the cavern and lurch drunkenly into a mammoth in full view of the cave-painters gathered outside. The painting then appeared on the walls first thing the next morning in what experts now agree was the very first recognisable issue of *Heat* magazine.

In the Roman era there were so many mad emperors it's

difficult to choose between them. For instance, Tiberius (AD 14–37) was paranoid about assassins and once attacked a fisherman (who he thought was trying to kill him) with a red mullet before scrubbing his body with a giant crab, while Nero (AD 54–68) sent the head of his wife to his new girlfriend as a gift (when surely a box of Ferrero Rocher would have worked just as well) and would dress up as an animal and attack victims at the Roman games. We best remember Nero, of course, for the Caffè Nero chain of coffee shops which he founded in direct competition with Starbucks, itself named after the Roman god of overpriced lattes, who would smite his enemies from the top of Mount Vesuvius with pointless froth and muffins. Nero, however, was out-mentalled by Elagabalus (AD 218–222) who once had 1,000 lb of cobwebs brought to him as proof of the glory of Rome. But it's Emperor Caligula (AD 37–41) who really takes the mental biscuit. Once, he went to invade Britain and stood on the shores of Normandy before realising he'd neglected to tell his army about his plan. When they eventually arrived, he forgot about Britain and instead declared war on the sea, making his troops walk up and down the beach to collect shells as proof of victory over the oceans. Actually, this peculiar act makes him mad, but at the same time quite sweet. Although not that sweet, because he then he had sex with a horse and made him into a Roman senator. Nutter.

Despite all this, the current record for Maddest Royal goes to PRINCE CHARLES, PRINCE OF WALES who famously conducts conversations with flowers, grows his own biscuits on some kind of organic farm in Cornwall and, if you'll recall the notorious 'Camillagate' tapes, wants to be reincarnated as Camilla Parker Bowles' tampon. This kind of bizarre behaviour kind of really makes you yearn for the old days.

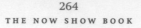

MOST SHADES OF HAIR
ON A HUMAN BODY

The record for the most shades of hair on a human body is currently held by the former Chancellor of the Exchequer – Alistair Darling – who, it is believed, has a different hair colour on each part of his body.

1 Head: white

2 Eyebrows: black

3 Chest: ginger

4 Stomach: auburn

5 Toes: strawberry blonde

6 Hands: werewolf grey

7 Legs: platinum blonde

8 Pubic area: bald

Obviously, this is all speculation, but that's good enough for Wikipedia so it is good enough for us. Anyway, it is far better left as speculation because there is only one way of finding out if any of this is true and I don't think any of us want to go there, do we? No, thought not.

As to the hair colours of the current Chancellor, we have few clues although there is a rumour that as the scion of a family of posh wallpaper manufacturers his chest hair has been fashioned to resemble the flock wallcovering popular in 1970s Indian restaurants.

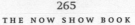

LONGEST TIME SPENT ON ONE DOMESTIC JOB BY BUILDERS

This was the staggering 18 MONTHS, 20 DAYS AND 6 HOURS that two 'blokes' took to complete a simple kitchen refurbishment at the home of Darren and Sharon Wood in Hinckley, Leicestershire. The original estimate was 10 days, but various factors led to the work going on 'a bit longer than expected'. Excuses used by the builders for the delay included 'These units need a special type of screw, mate, and B&Q have got none left' to 'Yeh, I would've got the sink in but my hammer had a cold' and 'Trouble is, we've got this other job on and anyway we're waiting on the sparky'. As a result of these delays, Mr and Mrs Wood were forced to cook on a camping stove in the hall and do the washing-up in the bathroom sink for the best part of a year and a half, which in itself is another record. Five years later, they are still missing the front of one drawer.

BUSIEST LANDSCAPE GARDENER

If you look through the National Trust guide, you will quickly discover that CAPABILITY BROWN apparently landscaped every stately home in Britain. He seems to have had a total landscaping monopoly, finding time to visit hundreds of posh houses and then issue instructions for digging, planting, damming, building artificial lakes and felling woods, and then buggering off to do the same thing somewhere else.

Quite how on earth he had time to landscape so many places is not clear. Historians now suspect that Capability Brown may in fact have been a franchise operation. Anyone could set up as a Capability Brown landscape gardener by paying 20 guineas in return for a certificate and a Capability periwig. Then you turned up with a sketch pad and a theodolite, issued Lord Whatsit and Lady Thingy with digging instructions and left. An advertisement was placed in *The Times* in 1761:

Fed up with those French-style parterres and formal beds? Then why not let Capability Brown dig it all up and make you an informal park with a lake and trees! Also built-in barbecues, decking and we'll even throw in a free shed! You only landscape your grounds once every few centuries, so use the best – Capability Brown is Britain's leading landscaper with over 70 future National Trust properties landscaped this year alone! So go on – send a messenger today!

MOST QUICKLY BROKEN NEW YEAR'S RESOLUTION

On the evening of 31 December 2006 Steve Grewcock of Hove, Sussex, vowed that he would stop smoking and lose weight, but by the end of 1 January 2007, after his ninth cigarette and 120th Quality Street chocolate, he simply gave up. On the morning of 1 January 2005, Dawn Gibbs of Nuneaton in Warwickshire, UK, claimed she would start going to the gym and possibly swimming but, 24 hours later as she sat on the sofa watching an afternoon re-run of *Babe The Sheep Pig* on BBC 1, she simply decided that, in actual fact, she wouldn't.

However, the breaking of this resolution is by no means the world's fastest, nor necessarily the most New Year-ish. In fact, the record for Most Quickly Broken Resolution goes to KIM JONG-IL of North Korea who once agreed to the United Nations Resolution number 1835 which re-affirmed the treaty on the non-proliferation of nuclear weapons and then, 20 minutes later, broke it by launching warheads into space and testing a bomb directly underneath some peasants. The speccy fat psycho.

MOST EFFECTIVE WAY TO COMMIT SUICIDE, FOR EXAMPLE IF YOU'RE A BANKER WHO'S LOST EVERYTHING

- Run a hosepipe into your car window. From a tap. And drown yourself.

- Guillotine yourself with the guillotine from the stationery cupboard.

- Move to Ipswich, get work as a prostitute and wait for the inevitable to happen.

- Dress in a panda costume and run in a zigzag fashion in front of Prince Philip.

❧ Draw a cartoon of Mohammed and have it published in a newspaper or book.

CARTOON REMOVED BY PUBLISHER ON GROUNDS OF HEALTH AND SAFETY

STUPIDEST THING A SOMALI PIRATE COULD DO WITH HIS BOOTY

While the world economy gets back to the Middle Ages, other aspects of modern life are following suit. For example, we now have pirates in the Gulf of Aden threatening the shipping lanes and hoping to take Saudi oil tankers. This is a little confusing. What are the pirates going to do with all their treasure? Normally they would bury it, but bury oil and all you have done is go back one stage in the refining process.

NB And if you try to bury the true amount of oil that is coming out of a broken pipeline, all you will do is make President Obama very cross.

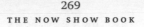

MOST LIVE ANIMALS INGESTED AT A SINGLE SITTING

This record was attempted by an unnamed old woman who, at some time unspecified in the past, swallowed a variety of animals and/or insects starting with a fly and going all the way up to a horse. Each animal was bigger than the last and to begin with it made sense as each creature was a predator of the previous one to be swallowed. For instance, after the fly, the old lady swallowed a spider which was followed by a bird, a cat and then a dog. At this point, the Record Adjudicator (TV's Norris McWhirter) noted that the old woman had swallowed a cow. While Mr McWhirter was well aware of the reason the old woman swallowed a fly (it was for the record attempt), he didn't know how she'd swallowed a cow. He reasoned that she'd swallowed the cow to catch the dog, after she'd swallowed the dog to catch the cat, which she'd swallowed in turn to catch the spider that wriggled and jiggled and tickled inside her. But according to the then rules, a cow isn't a natural predator of a dog and thus there was no earthly reason at all for swallowing it next. The old woman then compounded this error by swallowing a horse, leading Mr McWhirter to have her disqualified. Whereupon she died. Of course.

The current record for most animals ingested at a single sitting goes to an unmemorable ex-soap star on an unspecified series of the television show *I'm A Celebrity Get Me Out Of Here!*. The soap star ate a witchety grub, a testicle, a snake's guts and then either Ant or Dec. It was the one with the big forehead, if that helps.

MOST POINTLESS
HUMAN BEING

PARIS HILTON

NICEST
OLD MAN

There are many, many nice old men. Some sit in parks feeding the ducks, some are kindly vicars, while others are Sergeant Wilson and Private Godfrey out of *Dad's Army*. In a world where old people are quite often racist and/or drive too slowly in front of you in a Nissan Micra, it is always heartwarming to find a pensioner who isn't backward about coming forward with observations about the weather and some cake. In this category JON'S GREAT UNCLE ERN wins hands down. He lives in Nuneaton with Jon's Great Auntie Sylvie and they are quite possibly the most pleasant old couple you will ever meet. The runner-up is the man from the Werther's Original advert who forcefed his grandchild with buttery sweets. JH

WORLD'S LEAST DESIRABLE JOBS

- Robert Mugabe's anger-management coach

- Person in charge of moving Stonehenge to British Summer Time

- Michael Barrymore's pool cleaner

- Person employed to follow Elton John's pram around picking up the toys

- Person responsible for clearing up the morning after a war

- Anything in McDonald's

LONGEST SITTING IN A BATH OF BAKED BEANS

For some reason, charity events often involve endurance trials of people sitting in baths full of baked beans. It requires quite a lot of baked beans to fill a bath, and once they've been sat in, they're not edible, for health and safety reasons.

This makes it a poor choice for a charity event. It wastes both money and food. Imagine having to explain to a starving African that in order to buy them a spade, someone parked their arse in a month's worth of valuable protein and carbohydrates.

BIGGEST LIE
EVER TOLD

Opinions on this question divide along political lines. Right-wingers tend to regard 'global warming is man-made' as the biggest lie ever told; an advance on five years ago, when they claimed it wasn't happening at all. Left-wingers would tend to favour 'there is strong evidence that Iraq has weapons of mass destruction', a transatlantic porky issued by G. Bush and T. Blair, long after they knew that a) the evidence was very weak and b) it all came from one bloke who didn't like Saddam Hussein.

However, the true answer to this question lies away from contentious politics. In fact, it's not political in the slightest, and it's actually more irritating than either the Iraq war or the end of the world. The biggest lie ever told was told continuously throughout the mid-1980s and it was this:

CDS ARE VIRTUALLY INDESTRUBCTIBLE AND CANNOT GET SCRATCHED.

This was a massive, huge, staggering lie. Millions of people abandoned their lovingly built collections of vinyl albums on the basis of this outright fib. Vinyl albums would click and hiss and get little scratches on, but they would *still bloody play*.

CDs, as the world quickly realised, would also get little scratches on, and then *stop working*. CDs, of course, are now being killed off by downloads, and they *bloody deserve it*. They're *rubbish*. No, they don't hiss, but the music is so compressed that there's no top end to hear anyway. Apple have done us all a favour by giving us the means to abandon the nasty little silver glitch-mongering bird-scarers. The music industry is in big trouble nowadays, and they deserve it for lying about CDs being idestructible. The end can't come soon enough for the lying liars.

(See *BIGGEST LIES ON WIKIPEDIA*.)

WORST THINGS TO SAY AT A SECRET SERVICE INTERVIEW

From a survey of those no longer allowed in the MI6 building, the most career-threatening things to say were as follows:

- 'I can't just go to northern Pakistan now, I haven't had the injections.'

- 'This is nothing like *Spooks*.'

- 'I can't do that. It's illegal.'

- 'No way am I going in that sodding volcano.'

- 'Do you know what, destroy the world. I am so bored.'

- 'Easy with the Bollinger, it gives me terrible wind.'

- 'But, Felix, the last time I met you, you were a large black man.'

FUNNIEST CREATIONIST THEORY TO EXPLAIN AWAY AWKWARD FACT

Creationists believe Noah's Ark really existed and that one man and his family managed to collect two of every species, including all 30,000 species of moths, along with polar bears and penguins from parts of the world which nobody knew were there and would have taken months to reach anyway. Quite how he kept the polar bears happy on their long journey back to the baking hot Middle East nobody knows, least of all Creationists. The Ark, don't forget, had no propulsion system, so it couldn't go anywhere to collect anything – they had to come to Noah in order to embark. The pandas, for example, had to come thousands of miles from China. They ran out of bamboo halfway and had to live on sticks, which they hated.

Anyway, there's always been a bit of a problem with dinosaurs. If the dinosaurs all died out in the Flood (which is what they used to believe), then the Bible is wrong, since it clearly states that Noah took *all* the animals onto the Ark. Since the whole point of Creationism is that the Bible is all literally true, this clearly doesn't work. It was, therefore, necessary to work out how Noah could have got all the dinosaurs onto the Ark. Not only would they have taken up a lot of space (the brontosaurus alone requiring a whole deck, let alone two of them) – but many of them were ferocious carnivores, and would have frankly been quite tricky to contain, what with the Ark being built of wood and everything. They didn't manage to keep the T-Rex quiet in *Jurassic Park* even with metal fences and electricity. So Noah's chances of holding two of them in a home-made wooden boat would seem slim.

Anyway, Creationists thought long and hard about this and came up with the explanation – Noah took all the dinosaurs onto the Ark *but in egg form*. Yes, that's right – Noah went around and collected dinosaur *eggs* – two from each species. What's more, somehow he managed to make sure that the two eggs contained a male and a female. (Or maybe he didn't, which is why the dinosaurs all died out. When the eggs hatched out they were all blokes.)

So just to repeat that – because I'm not making this up – Noah, a man from the eastern Mediterranean around 4,000 years ago, collected two eggs from every species of dinosaur and stored them all in a big wooden boat. Forty per cent of the adult population of the United States, the world's leading technological superpower, genuinely believe this to be historical fact.

Jesus H. Christ!

MOST UNFORTUNATE TATTOO

It used to be that you knew where you were with tattoos. If someone had one then they were either a sailor or a Hell's Angel, or the sort of person that thinks an unmuzzled Rottweiler with a record of mauling babies makes an ideal family pet. These people had 'love' and 'hate' tattooed on their knuckles (which would often rub off on the ground as they walked), anchors on their forearms like Popeye, dragons on their chests like idiots or their girlfriend's name written on their shoulders – usually one of many names with the ones above it half-heartedly crossed out. That sort of romantic gesture must really impress your loved one, mustn't it? Why not carry your notched headboard around with you as well, along with the AIDS you've caught from crossing the names out yourself with a borrowed needle?

When I was growing up, home-made tattoos were all the rage. Once, at school, Paul 'Bones' Jones made one on his own arm using the point of a compass that he kept dipping in a bottle of Quink. He claimed that the resulting mess spelt out the name of his then girlfriend Penny (she was my ex, as it happens, but that's another story) but what it actually said was ▬▬▬▬ . This was because he was a) right-handed and had done it with his left hand and b) seemingly unaware that tattoos made with maths implements and fountain pen ink don't work. And, far from being impressed with his cack-handed declaration of love, Penny was livid and dumped him. I was secretly pleased.

Tattoos have moved on since then. David Beckham popularised them sometime in the early 2000s when he had various mystical symbols inked up his limbs and his child's name written across his neck in Hindi or some such. This was unfortunate because it was later revealed that bits of it were spelt wrong and, as no one has ever invented tattoo Tippex, he's stuck with it even though it looks stupid. Much like he is with Victoria. Or 'VICTHTORAI' as it probably says halfway up his arm.

Of course, tattoos are by no means the preserve of the thick male. Some women are quite fond of tattoos too, but pictures of anchors or dragons are not for them. No, these days, various Celtic symbols are the skin art du jour, ranging from the stupid circle on the ankle (*comm. abbr.:* 'Slag Tag'. See *UNDERAGE MOTHERS: WORLD'S CHAVVIEST*) to the slightly more ornate one on the female lower back that comes into view just above the thong every time a girl bends over. The correct name for this tattoo design is 'bum antlers'.

A most unfortunate tattooing incident occurred in 2004 when Kelly Holmes ran to victory in the Olympics, a victory celebrated by Kelly Holmes fan Emma Fitch (22) of Tonbridge, Kent, UK who had a picture of the athlete-ess tattooed on her back. What she ended up with was something that looked less like a tattoo and more like something done in felt-tip pen by the most inept tattooist ever to pick up a needle. And to add insult to injury, 'Kelly Holmes' was spelt wrong, the 'L' being missing from 'Holmes'. From this evidence, I think we can work out what eventual career path Paul 'Bones' Jones followed after he left school.

While these examples are worthy of note, in fact the world's most unfortunate tattoo was the French dwarf actor Hervé Villechaize who played 'Tattoo' in the 1970s TV series *Fantasy Island*. He committed suicide in 1993. And that is unfortunate. JH

WORLD'S LONGEST QUEUE

The world's longest queue was long thought to be at Terminal 5 of Heathrow Airport during its opening week in 2008, when 782 passengers lined up near a check-in desk to await their turn to punch British Airways Chief Executive Willie Walsh in the face. However a subsequent line of people trying to use a self-service checkout at Sainsbury's in Northampton in June 2010 grew to number an estimated 3,456 when the machine found an 'unexpected item in the bagging area' (see *ITEMS IN THE BAGGING AREA, MOST UNEXPECTED*). As a result, the system ground to a halt as both robotised contraption and human staff raced to find out just what it was. As all the other checkouts were closed, the line of people tutting eventually grew to encompass most of the store, the car park and surrounding area before a Saturday boy finally identified the unexpected item as a tomato. Even post-analysis, the queue still grew by another 25% as the old lady whose tomato it was insisted on paying with change.

Another notably large queue formed in a Manchester branch of Costa Coffee in August 2010, when the man at the front couldn't decide what size cappuccino to have.

DULLEST CHURCH SERVICE

This was at St John's Methodist Church in Nuneaton, Warwickshire, in September 1981. This record was adjudicated personally by Jon Holmes, who was lured to the church under false pretences after his mum told him they were going to 'the Harvest Festival'. Jon took this to mean he would be going to an outdoor autumn concert, possibly with full sets from that year's big chart hitters the Human League and Adam and the Ants, with a possible acoustic set from Howard Jones. Instead, all that was on offer at the so-called festival site was a handful of old-age pensioners, quite a boring vicar and an out-of-date tin of cling peaches in an old shoebox that Jon's mum had lined with green crêpe paper.

Jon's disappointment was compounded when, despite a

sermon containing promises of 'God's bounty', there was not a single Bounty to be seen. The closest anything came, as verified by those present, was a six pack of Blue Ribands, which is, at best, the poor man's chocolate treat, given that the wafer-to-milk-chocolate ratio is all wrong (see *CHOCOLATE, MOST BORINGEST*). And anyway, they weren't for general consumption because they were 'a gift for an old people's home', according to Jon's mum as she slapped his hand away. The service itself went on for what felt like eight years and incorporated some of the world's most annoying hymns. These are the ones that fool the singer into thinking they are short but then some unknown church law demands that you sing the first verse again in between every single one of the others, making it last six times as long as it reasonably ought to.

Jon has more or less consistently stayed away from festivals ever since, just in case Glastonbury, rather than being the world's greatest celebration of contemporary performing arts and music, instead turns out to be a lengthy Christening service in a draughty chapel.

BIGGEST FRAUD

The world's biggest fraud was that perpetrated by American financier BERNARD MADOFF. No one could have seen it coming, apparently. Er, hello, the man's name was Madoff, and that's what he did, Madoff with billions. I'm not sure anyone who invested with him can really complain, he just did exactly what it says on the tin. He might as well have called himself

Ivor Bigscam, or Mr Dona-Runner. More surprisingly, this was
a fraud which took in some of the world's most sophisticated
financiers, none of them made even the slightest bit suspicious
by the fact that while the global economy was shrinking, the
Madoff fund consistently returned 12% year after year. In a world
of sophisticated mathematical models, the equation, for them,
seemed quite simple:

**Unlikely level of returns + no questions asked =
profits for everyone**

Until they found themselves $50bn down, and discovered that
they had been victims of a massive pyramid-selling scam called
a Ponzi Scheme. This is, of course, not to be confused with a
poncy scheme, which might for example be a plan to go to
Glyndebourne armed with a picnic of foie gras and quails' eggs,
because one 'simply must see this production of *Giulio Cesare*'.
A Ponzi Scheme is illegal, a poncy scheme is merely pretentious.

WORLD'S STUPIDEST CONSPIRACY THEORY

The fulfilment, in 1969, of President Kennedy's promise to
land a man on the moon and bring him safely back to earth
'before this decade is out' is one of the best examples of
America's energy, determination and vision. The fact that half
of all Americans think it was all faked is, therefore, all the more
disappointing, unless you enjoy laughing at stupid Americans.
Here is just a shortlist of reasons why this 'theory' is flawed:

a) Technically tricky . . .

If there hadn't been any radio signals coming from the moon, the Russians would have known about it. And they would have said something, probably along the lines of 'the capitalist running-dogs of America are faking their moon-landing and we can very easily prove it'. They didn't do this.

b) Why go back?

The theory says that the landing had to happen in 1969 in order to keep Kennedy's 'before the decade is out' promise. The Americans then went back to the moon *another five times*, plus one failed mission (Apollo 13). Really, if they'd got away with faking a moon landing, then faking *five more* is just taking the piss.

c) What was the point?

America could have swallowed hard and said to the world, 'Landing on the moon is proving more technically difficult than we thought. It is also too expensive. We are reluctantly postponing the project.' But no. Instead they decide to carry out a massive conspiracy, involving the whole of NASA, the US government, the military and the media, creating the risk of a national humiliation that would stain the country forever. Yet shortly afterwards, a US President is forced to resign – just for bugging people's offices. Good job they didn't find out you also faked the moon landings, eh, Mr Nixon? Explain *that* to David Frost!

The kind of people who think the Apollo landings were faked are the same people who think the US government deliberately flew unmanned drone aircraft into the World Trade Center. In other words, idiots.

WORST DECISION
EVER MADE

History is littered with bad decisions. Lord Cardigan at the Charge of the Light Brigade, President Johnson sending troops into Vietnam and Peter Fincham, the then-controller of BBC1, giving Davina McCall her own chat show. Hindsight, like chocolate fudge cake, is a wonderful thing, but there are many contenders for the very worst decision ever made. Some are listed below:

JOHN F. KENNEDY, 1963 'It's a nice day, let's take the soft top.'

PILOT OF CHALLENGER SPACE SHUTTLE, 1986 'It's cool, by all means let the woman drive.'

KING HAROLD, 1066 'What about if I stand here and look upwards? Do you think it'll look good on the tapestry?'

SENIOR EXECUTIVE, ROYAL BANK OF SCOTLAND, 3 MARCH 2006 'I suggest we invest in sub-prime mortgage bonds. They're a dead cert.'

In Spring 1941, Adolf Hitler called his military commanders to a conference in Berlin and announced that he was giving up any intention of invading Britain, preventing the island from becoming a base to launch a re-invasion of occupied Europe. Instead, Germany would attack Russia. Until Royal Bank of Scotland came along, this was almost certainly the worst decision ever made.

THE TEN THINGS YOU SHOULD MAKE THE LEAST EFFORT TO DO BEFORE YOU DIE

1 Queue at a bus stop in the rain.

2 Eat a two-day-old three-bean salad from a Tupperware box.

3 Drive between junctions 12 and 15 of the M25.

4 Get a verruca.

5 Swim in a lock on the Grand Union Canal.

6 Be taught by nuns.

7 Visit Charnock Richard Services and have the Cumberland sausage.

8 Watch QVC.

9 Fly TAROM – the Romanian National Airline.

10 Read this book right to the end.